The Skills in English Course

Level 3

Part A

Resources Book

Terry Phillips and Anna Phillips

Garnet EDUCATION

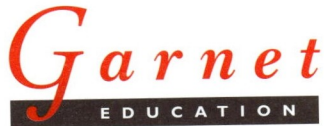

Published by
Garnet Publishing Ltd.
8 Southern Court
South Street
Reading RG1 4QS, UK

© 2007 Garnet Publishing Ltd.

The right of Terry Phillips and Anna Phillips to be identified as the authors of this work has been asserted by them in accordance with the Copyright, Designs and Patents Act 1988.

All rights reserved.
No part of this publication may be reproduced, stored in a retrieval system, or transmitted in any form or by any means, electronic, mechanical, photocopying, recording or otherwise, without the prior permission of the Publisher. Any person who does any unauthorized act in relation to this publication may be liable to criminal prosecution and civil claims for damages.

ISBN-13: 978-1-85964-933-6

British Library Cataloguing-in-Publication Data
A catalogue record for this book is available from the British Library.

Production

Project managers:	Maggie MacIntyre, Richard Peacock
Editorial team:	John Bates, Emily Clarke, Natalie Griffith, Sarah Margetts, Katharine Mendelsohn, Nicky Platt, Lucy Thompson
Art director:	David Rose
Design:	Mark Slader
Illustration:	Beehive Illustration (Dave Bowyer/John Dunne/Janos Jantner/Mark Ruffle/Simon Rumble/Pete Smith/Pulsar Studio/Roger Wade Walker), David Stevens, Janette Hill, Doug Nash, Karen Rose, Ian West
Photography:	Apple Computers, Inc., Corbis (Chris Lisle/Stapleton Collection/Dennis Marsico/Wolfgang Kaehler/Hulton-Deutsch Collection/ Bettman/The Scotsman/Underwood & Underwood/L. Clarke/Rob Lewine/Ariel Skelley/Jim Cummins/Norbert Schaefer), Digital Vision, Flat Earth, Image Source, Photodisc, Istockphoto, Pixtal, Mary Evans Picture Library, NOAA Picture Library
Audio production:	Matinée Sound & Vision Ltd. and John Green TEFL Tapes

Garnet Publishing wishes to thank the following for their assistance in the development of this project:
Dr Abdullah Al Khanbashi, Abderrazak Ben Hamida, Maxine Gillway, Susan Boylan and the Level 3 team at UGRU, UAE University.

Every effort has been made to trace the copyright holders and we apologize in advance for any unintentional omissions. We will be happy to insert the appropriate acknowledgements in any subsequent editions.

Study Skills Success software © Clarity Language Consultants Ltd 2006 www.clarity.com.hk

Google™ is a trademark of Google Inc.

Printed and bound
in Lebanon by International Press

Resources Book

Contents

Reading Resources

Teaching and Learning	4
L1 and the LAD	6
Nature … or Nurture?	8
Are Identical Twins the Key to Understanding Nature and Nurture?	10
An Interesting Job Is Better than a Well-Paid One	12
Managers and Workers Just Need SOMething to Live For	14
Red Sky at Night. Did They Get It Right?	16
Forecasting Today – Science or Art?	18
Petroleum	20

Grammar Skills — 24

Transcript — 39

Word Lists
- Thematic Word List — 56
- Alphabetical Word List — 58

CHAPTER ONE

Teaching and Learning

In this book, you are going to learn a great deal about teaching. However, before we concentrate on teaching, we must think about learning. In this first chapter, we will study the words 'teaching' and 'learning'. If you remember the exact meanings of these words, it will help you before, during and after each lesson.

Teaching means helping people to learn, or telling or showing people how to learn. Teaching needs at least two people: a teacher and a learner. These two people work together on a particular subject so that learning takes place.

The meaning of the word 'learning' changes according to what you are trying to learn. In some cases, it means acquiring or improving your knowledge of a subject. In other cases, it means acquiring or improving your skill at doing something. Sometimes it just means memorizing information, rote learning or learning by heart. Rote learning lessons are useful when a subject has a lot of facts, like history and geography; or formulas, like science and maths; or vocabulary, like foreign languages. In some special situations, like management training, learning means changing your behaviour.

Learning only needs one person, the learner. With self-study, there is no teacher. With distance training, the teacher may be in a different town or even a different country. A learner, in other words, does not always need a teacher, but a teacher often makes learning more efficient.

Teaching is about helping people to learn. The key word here is 'learn'. It does not matter how much teaching you do, if nobody learns anything!

You sometimes hear a teacher say: 'I taught them the present perfect today,' or 'how to do long division' or 'the names of all the presidents of the United States.' Does the teacher mean, 'I went into the classroom and talked about the present perfect, long division, US presidents'? Or does the teacher mean, 'They learnt how to use the present perfect, how to do long division, how to remember the presidents'? A lesson must always have a learning aim. We can plan a lesson on paper, but it will not work in the classroom if it does not have a clear learning aim. You need to decide the learning aim before each lesson, and keep it in mind during the lesson. After the lesson, you can use your learning aim to assess the lesson. Ask yourself the question – did the students achieve the learning aim?

It is difficult to write a learning aim from the definition of learning above. It is easier if we turn the definition of learning into questions.
1 What new knowledge or skills will the students acquire in this lesson?
2 What will the students know, or be able to do, better at the end of the lesson?
3 What will the students know by heart by the end of the lesson?
4 How will the students behave in future? Usually, only one of the questions will be relevant for a particular lesson. If your aim answers Question 1, you are going to teach a Presentation lesson. If it answers Question 2, you are going to teach a Practice or Production lesson. What about Questions 3 and 4? In both cases, the lessons will be Presentation, with perhaps some Practice. Production will come later, in a test or in behaviour in the real world.

L1 *and the* LAD

HOW DO WE LEARN A LANGUAGE? It is a difficult question to answer, partly because it is not really one question, but two. The first question is: *How do we learn our first language?* The second question is: *How do we learn a second or foreign language?*

Why do we need to separate the questions? The reason is that there is a huge difference between learning a first language, which linguists sometimes call L1, and learning a second one (L2). We all learn the language of our childhood environment, but only a few of us go on to learn other languages.

Linguists use special words to talk about L1. There are words for the first language itself, the first-language learner and the learning process that a child uses. First language is called mother tongue, presumably because a child usually learns the language that his or her mother speaks. The first-language learner is called a native speaker. The process of learning the first language is called acquisition. This is the noun from *acquire*, which the dictionary defines as *get for oneself* or *come into possession of*. In other words, acquisition has a feeling of getting without trying.

Does a child have to try to learn his or her mother tongue? It depends whether you are talking about the spoken language or the written language. Acquisition of the spoken language seems to happen without any actual teaching. Mothers correct children when they make mistakes, but usually the corrections are factual, not grammatical or to do with pronunciation. Somehow, a child learns to communicate with other children from the same speech group. It is a different story with the written language. In this case, in all cultures there is direct teaching of the skills, but many children fail to learn them. In fact, there are 870 million illiterate adults in the world today. That's nearly 15 per cent of the world's population.

Are all children fluent in their mother tongue? Again it depends which language you are talking about. The answer for spoken language is yes. A child at the age of six or seven knows his or her first language far better than most non-native speakers will ever learn it. They usually know very little about the grammar or the pronunciation rules, but they are experts at communicating day-to-day needs, hopes and fears. Scientists explain this by saying that all children are born with a language acquisition device (or LAD) that works up to about the age of five or six. Above that age, the LAD switches off and we must *learn* a second language rather than *acquire* it.

What about language *learning*? This process seems to be very different from language acquisition. Even when an adult lives in a foreign country and is exposed to the language in its natural environment, language learning may not take place. It seems that a language learner needs to study the grammar and the pronunciation rules and to make a conscious effort to learn. For centuries, language teaching has reflected this focus on form. Language teachers have spent most of their time on grammatical rules and pronunciation exercises.

Is there really an LAD? Scientists cannot prove that children have a language acquisition device. It is possible that the real difference between acquisition and learning lies in the focus of the exercise. Acquisition focuses on communication. The child wants to communicate with the mother; the mother wants to communicate with the child. Language teaching, as noted above, has traditionally focused on form, on what the language should look and sound like. Perhaps if language teaching focused only on communication, we could acquire a foreign language as easily as we acquire our mother tongue. There is more focus on communication now in the language classroom, but we are still a long way from producing fluent speakers at any age.

Nature ... or Nurture?

WHY HAVE YOU GOT BROWN EYES and not blue? Why do you weigh 68 kilograms and not 60? What accounts for your level of intelligence? Why do you behave the way you do? Most people think they have inherited their eye colour, but what about the rest? Even psychologists and geneticists do not agree about the other points.

There has been a debate about this issue for many years. The question is: Do features like behaviour, appearance, health and intelligence come from our parents and grandparents? Or do they come from the way we grow up, the things that happen to us in our childhood? In other words, are they from nature, or nurture? This, in psychology, is called the nature-nurture problem. Nature, in this context, means things we were born with, and nurture means things that we have learned or that have developed in a certain way because of the environment that we live in.

It is easy to find an answer with plants. You can cut a plant into three equal pieces, put each part in a different environment and see what happens. The three plants must have the same DNA, so any differences in development must come from the environment.

Nowadays, we can even find an answer with animals. We can clone animals, which means we can produce genetically identical animals from the mother's DNA. We can then raise them in different environments.

We are unable to use either of these approaches with human beings. It is physically impossible to cut one individual into three pieces

The Jim Twins

The famous 'Jim Twins' were called Jim Springer and Jim Lewis. They were adopted in 1940 and reunited 39 years later, in 1979. Psychologist Thomas Bouchard studied them and found some incredible similarities between the attitudes and behaviour of the two men.

The first similarity must just be coincidence. They were both named Jim by their adoptive parents.

Bouchard was unsurprised to discover that they had identical medical histories. This included migraine headaches from the age of 18. We might expect identical twins to have identical bodies and therefore suffer from the same illnesses.

However, some of the other similarities were unbelievable. Both had married twice, the first time to women named Linda and the second time to women named Betty, and they both had one son called James. It is not unusual for American fathers to name their first son after themselves, but why did Jim Springer choose

and bring the three pieces up differently. Most people would say it is immoral to clone humans. It is certainly unethical to experiment with children – deliberately putting one child in a loving environment, for example, and another in an uncaring one, to see what happens.

We cannot generalize from the results with plants or cloned animals to say anything useful about human beings. The environment of a plant or an animal is much simpler than the environment of a baby or a young child.

So, where can we look for evidence about the effect of nature and nurture on people? The answer is: twin studies. These are cases of identical twins who were separated at or just after birth and then brought up in different environments.

Through these studies and other research, scientists have discovered many interesting facts. It seems that physical features like eye colour and hair colour are nearly all due to hereditary factors, but that weight, for example, is unlikely to depend on heredity. Diet is much more important. Height, on the other hand, is largely inherited. Scientists have also discovered that certain psychiatric disorders are inherited and so are certain diseases or the susceptibility to certain diseases.

Factors like intelligence and personality are less easy to attribute to nature or nurture. One problem with intelligence is that there is a lot of disagreement about how to measure it. IQ tests often do not take into account educational or cultural differences. However, current thinking is that we inherit between 60% and 80% of the type of intelligence measured by IQ texts.

What about negative traits? A recent study in Denmark has discovered that many children of criminals also developed criminal or antisocial tendencies, even when they were adopted and brought up in a completely different environment. Will people in future be able to claim that their genes made them commit illegal or irresponsible acts?

In conclusion, it seems that we can attribute individual differences between people partly to nature and partly to nurture.

Allen for the boy's second name while Jim Lewis chose Alan? Both of the twins had dogs named Toy. They both drank the same kind of drinks, they both smoked the same brand of cigarettes and they both drove the same type of car. They both liked carpentry and made things around the house, including an identical bench round a very similar tree in each twin's garden. They hated baseball and loved stock car racing. They both bit their nails. They both worked for some time as a deputy sheriff, which is a kind of local police officer. They were both average to poor students at school and both had the same political views.

Perhaps the strangest similarity was in their behaviour towards their respective wives. They both left love notes for their wives around the house.

Bouchard went on to work with other reunited identical twins in his research centre in the twin capital cities of Minnesota, Minneapolis and St. Pauls.

Bouchard's work seems to show that genes are much more powerful in shaping our behaviour and attitudes than we used to think.

Are Identical Twins the Key to Understanding Nature and Nurture?

This week, *Science Today* talks to Professor Andrew Morgan, a geneticist, about his work and the nature or nurture debate.

ST: What are you working on at the moment?

Prof: Well, my main area of research is identical twins. This type of twin results from the division of a single egg, and so the twins are identical in appearance and in their biochemistry.

ST: So all identical twins are absolutely identical in every way?

Prof: Well, things can happen in their development to produce anomalies, but often they are photocopies of each other, apart from their fingerprints!

ST: In their development? Do you mean before or after birth?

Prof: Before birth.

ST: And do identical twins grow up to be identical in behaviour and attitudes?

Prof: In many cases they do, but of course, they usually grow up in the same environment, so they are unlikely to have different behaviour and attitudes.

ST: Yes, although of course, two children who

Science Today Issue 256

grow up in the same family are often dissimilar in their behaviour and attitudes.

Prof: That's true, but psychologists think that is related to their age rank in the family.

ST: You mean, the eldest child develops in a different way from the youngest?

Prof: Exactly. With identical twins, of course, they are the same age, so the age rank factor is irrelevant.

ST: So twins growing up together are unhelpful as far as the nature or nurture debate is concerned?

Prof: That's right. The most useful kind of research is when identical twins were separated at birth and then brought up in completely different environments.

ST: Are there many cases like that?

Prof: Well, they are uncommon, but we know of about 25 cases. Perhaps the most famous are the Jim Twins. I didn't do any research on them myself, but apparently, although they grew up in very different environments, they were very similar in attitude and behaviour. For example, they both hated baseball and loved stock car racing.

ST: That's strange. We often think likes and dislikes come from our upbringing.

Prof: Indeed. People say: My dad took me to watch baseball when I was five and I fell in love with the game.

ST: What about your own research into identical twins?

Prof: Well, the strangest thing I have discovered is about phobias.

ST: You mean irrational fear of spiders and things?

Prof: Yes. My research suggests that many phobias are inherited.

ST: I thought phobias were environmental in origin.

Prof: Yes, so did I, but I discovered that twins who were separated at birth often shared really strange phobias. For example, one set of twins was terrified of escalators!

ST: They were frightened of moving stairs?

Prof: Yes. Neither twin would set foot on an escalator!

ST: What else have you discovered?

Prof: Well, there are some kinds of characteristics, like imagination, susceptibility to stress, leadership ability, that are inherited. But other traits, for example orderliness, aggression and sociability, are mostly caused by the home environment.

ST: What is the strangest thing you discovered in your study of twins separated at birth?

Prof: Well, I'm studying a set of twins at the moment. One child was brought up in Spain and the other in Germany. When I traced them, they were wearing identical clothes, both had small moustaches and both had the same strange habits: they both kept several elastic bands on their left wrists and read books and magazines from the back to the front.

ST: So, as a result of your research, where do you stand on the nature-nurture debate?

Prof: Well, my studies show that hereditary factors are very important in the shaping of a person.

Science Today Issue 256

An Interesting Job Is Better than a Well-Paid One

Both women and men would rather have an interesting job than a highly paid one. That is the conclusion of researchers, following a recent survey of public opinion. The survey involved more than 3,000 men and women across the United Kingdom.

The workers were shown a list of 14 factors related to work. They were asked to say which of these factors was important to them. The researchers, from the Business Studies Faculty of the University of Wessex, found that most workers regarded pay and overtime as less important than job security and work satisfaction.

Of those questioned, 59 per cent of men and an amazing 67 per cent of women said that it was important to have an interesting job. It was the top factor for women and second only to a secure job for men.

Another interesting result was the importance that both men and women gave to doing something worthwhile. This was in third place for both. This may be a reaction to the view of some managers that workers, particularly in factories, are just part of the machines.

Just two places lower for men (three places lower for women) was the importance of being able to organize one's own work. This suggests that workers want to have a say in how they do their jobs. This is in line with other studies that have shown that work stress is highest in jobs where the worker has little or no control over the organization of his or her work.

One result will come as a surprise to many people who have written about motivation in the workplace. Being recognized for good work is generally regarded as very important for workers. However, men put this factor in 12th place, while women only rated it slightly more important, putting it in 10th place.

Although men and women agreed on the most important and the least important points, there were clear gender differences in the centre of the table. The most striking example was in rating the importance of working for a boss that you respect. Women put this factor in fourth place, whereas men put it tenth. Perhaps this is because women are often not respected by their (male) managers. Having flexible working hours was much more important to women (32 per cent) – presumably because of child care concerns – whereas only 23 per cent of men thought this was important. On the other hand, working for a successful company was important for men but hardly rated as a factor for women. Apparently, men get some of their social status from the company they work for. Similarly, having a chance of promotion was much more important for men than for woman – 29 per cent, compared with 21 per cent. Possibly, men get more of their job satisfaction from their level in a company.

How can you make a job interesting? According to some management gurus, you cannot give people boring work and then try to organize it in an interesting way. You must make jobs interesting in themselves, then people will be motivated to do them.

How can you make a job worthwhile? Management consultants suggest that you must make sure that workers see the value of their contribution to the whole work process.

The results of this survey should make some managers think again about the way they manage. Interesting, worthwhile jobs seem to be more motivating than well-paid ones.

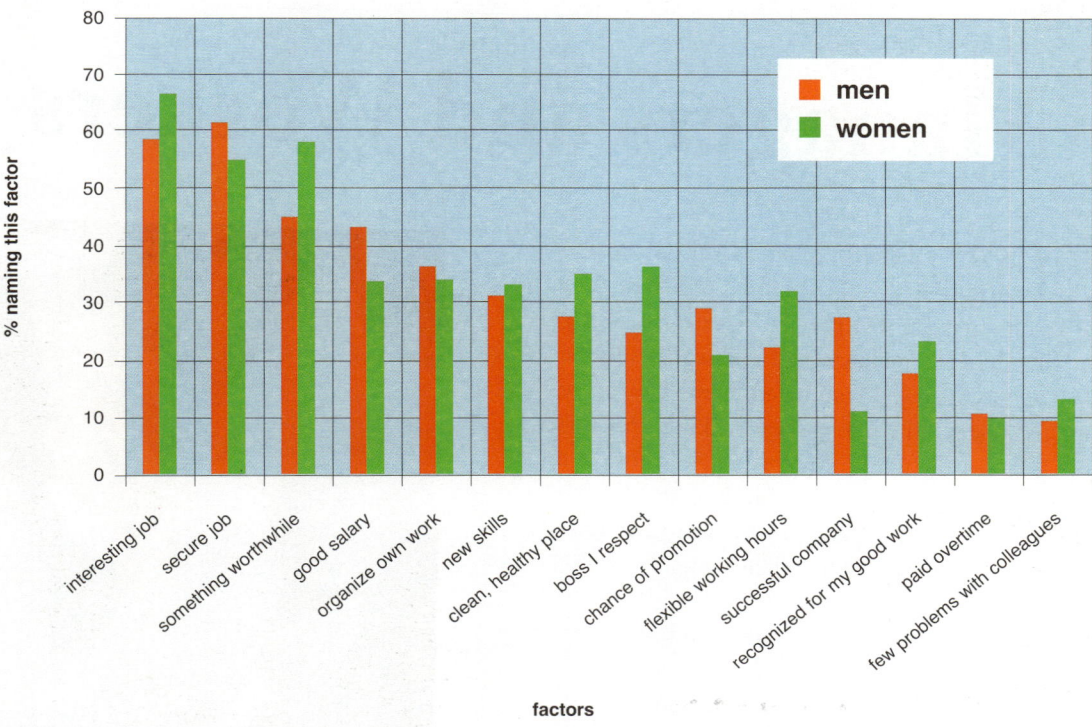

Figure 1: *Comparison of important job factors for men and women*

Table 1: *Rank order of job factors for men and women*

	Men	
	It is important to me to …	
1	have a secure job.	61
2	have an interesting job.	59
3	do something worthwhile.	45
4	have a good salary.	42
5	be able to organize my own work.	36
6	learn new skills.	31
7	have a chance of promotion.	29
8	work in a clean, healthy place.	28
9	work for a successful company.	28
10	work for a boss I respect.	25
11	have flexible working hours.	23
12	be recognized for my good work.	18
13	be able to do paid overtime.	11
14	have few problems with colleagues.	9

	Women	
	It is important to me to …	
1	have an interesting job.	67
2	have a secure job.	55
3	do something worthwhile.	48
4	work for a boss I respect.	37
5	work in a clean, healthy place.	35
6	be able to organize my own work.	34
7	have a good salary.	33
8	learn new skills.	33
9	have flexible working hours.	32
10	be recognized for my good work.	23
11	have a chance of promotion.	21
12	have few problems with colleagues.	14
13	work for a successful company.	11
14	be able to do paid overtime.	10

Good Management Journal Issue 154

Managers and Workers Just

DO WORKERS AND MANAGERS HAVE THE SAME NEEDS AT WORK? A recent study suggests that they do. The study, which involved 30 managers and 300 workers in the Wessex area, was conducted by the University of Wessex. The results show striking similarities between the needs of managers and those of their workers. However, they also show that both managers and workers are unable to accurately assess the needs of the other group.

Managers were asked to rate eight statements of need in order of importance for them. Then they were asked to rate the same needs in order of importance for their workers. Similarly, workers were asked to rate the eight statements for themselves and their managers.

The results show that the self-assessed needs of managers and workers are very similar. Both groups put security and an interesting job at the top, both put status and having a good time at the bottom. Both felt that achieving something worthwhile and making a lot of money was quite important.

When we compare the managers' statements of their own needs with their view of workers' needs, we find some big differences. The managers put having a good time at the bottom of their list of priorities, but in third place for workers. Presumably, they feel that workers want to avoid work, whereas they are prepared to work hard. Conversely, they put achieving something worthwhile in third place for themselves and bottom for the workers. Apparently, they believe that workers are not interested in their work – they work to live, as the saying goes, rather than living to work.

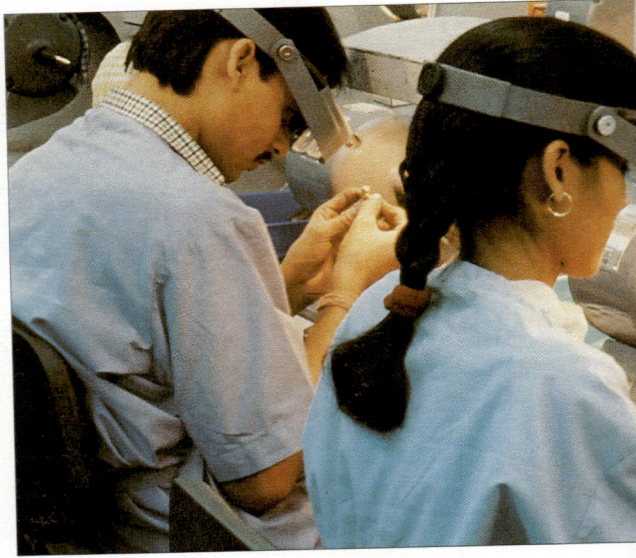

Figure 1: *Managers' and workers' assessment of own needs*

Good Management Journal Issue 154

Need SOMething to Live For

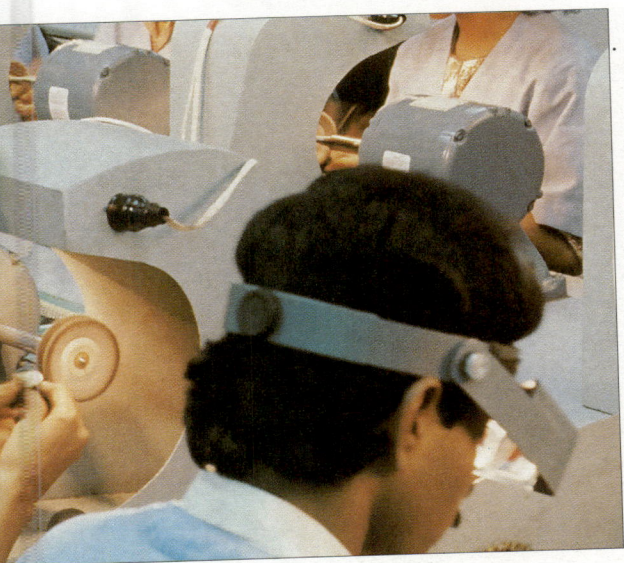

Table 1: *Managers' assessment of workers' needs*

	Managers' own needs	Managers' view of workers	Difference
to do something interesting	1	5	-4
to be secure	2	1	1
to achieve something worthwhile	3	8	-5
to make a lot of money	4	2	2
to be independent	5	6	-1
to be liked	6	4	2
to have a high status	7	7	0
to have a good time	8	3	5

Table 2: *Workers' assessment of managers' needs*

	Workers' own needs	Workers' view of managers	Difference
to be secure	1	4	-3
to do something interesting	2	7	-5
to make a lot of money	3	1	2
to achieve something worthwhile	4	6	-2
to be independent	5	5	0
to be liked	6	8	-2
to have a good time	7	2	5
to have a high status	8	3	5

We find the same discrepancies when we compare the workers' statements of their own needs with their view of managers' needs. The workers put having a good time in second place for the managers (after making a lot of money) and doing something interesting in seventh place. Perhaps this reflects a 'fat cat' view of managers – not interested in the job, only interested in making money for themselves.

The similarity between the self-assessed needs of the two groups surprised the managers and the workers, but not the researchers who carried out the study. 'We have known for some time that the needs of managers and workers are basically the same,' says Mike Gibbs, Head of the Business Studies Faculty at the university. 'Most people want to enjoy their work and they want to achieve something worthwhile, whether they are sweeping the streets or managing a multinational company. Unfortunately, managers often don't recognize workers' real needs, and the same is true of workers. Possibly this leads to the 'them and us' attitude you get in many large companies.'

How can we get managers and workers to see eye-to-eye on needs? Mike Gibbs thinks we have to remember that managers and workers are people first, employees second. 'It is not surprising we have the same needs,' he says, 'because we are all people. People need three things in their lives. We call it SOM: Security – safety for now and the future; Opportunity – to do something interesting and challenging; and Meaning – to achieve something worthwhile.'

So just remember SOM when you think about SOMebody else at work. They probably have the same needs as you.

Red Sky at Night.

HOW CAN WE PREDICT THE WEATHER TOMORROW IN A PARTICULAR PLACE? Throughout history, Man has tried to perform this useful task, and has succeeded, with greater and greater accuracy. Today, weather forecasts for the next 24 hours can be very accurate, and even five-day forecasts from the Meteorological Office are right more often than they are wrong.

In this, the first of two articles, we are going to look at how it all started. We are going to consider how accurate weather forecasting was in the days before modern data-collection devices. In the next article, we will look at developments in meteorology in the last 50 years.

Origins of meteorology

In the 5th century BCE, the Ancient Greeks were interested in natural events that happened in the atmosphere, like clouds and rain. They were particularly interested in shooting stars. They gave the name *meteors* to the objects that fell into the Earth's atmosphere and burnt up, and they called the study of such phenomena *meteorology*. In 400 BCE, Aristotle wrote a book that was called *Meteorologica*. It contained his thoughts about rain, cloud, mist, snow, hail, wind, thunder and lightning that were based on his first-hand observations. Over time, the title of Aristotle's book came to be used for the study of weather and particularly for the skill of weather forecasting.

We now call a lot of early forecasting *weather lore*. For example, in England and many other countries in the Northern Hemisphere there is a famous saying:

Red sky at night,
Shepherd's delight.
Red sky in the morning,
Shepherd's warning.

In other words, if the sky is red at sunset, the next day will be fine, whereas if the sky is red in the morning, the day will be stormy. It may sound like an old wives' tale, but this kind of weather lore was clearly based on observation of what actually happened after a red sky at sunset or sunrise. Other observations were based on the behaviour of animals. For instance:

Cows lying on the hay,
We shall have rain today.

When the donkey starts to bray,
It will rain and rain that day.

Seagull, seagull, on the sand,
It's never good weather
When you're on the land.

Some people found indications of the day's weather in the direction of the wind, the position of the clouds or when rain arrived:

When the wind is from the south,
The rain's in its mouth.

The higher the clouds,
The better the weather.

Wind before the rain,
Turn and work again.
Rain then the wind,
Pack up and go in.

Rain before seven,
Clear by eleven.

These pieces of weather lore predicted the weather in one place in the next six to 12 hours. We could call it *here and now* forecasting. However, observation can also assist in making longer-range predictions. In the 14th century, people in a few places started to make careful

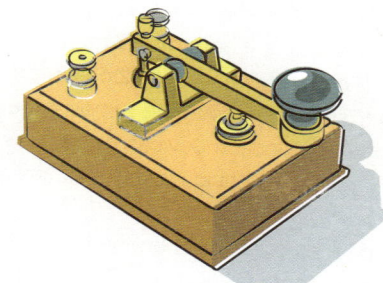

Did They Get It Right?

records of the weather on every day of the year. This led to *repetition* forecasting, which assumed that the weather *this* June, for example, would be the same as the weather *last* June. When people had kept records for several years, they could begin to look for patterns over longer periods, and more weather lore appeared. There is a famous piece of weather lore from the 16th century that English people quote every year:

> Swithin's Day, if it does rain,
> For forty days it will remain;
> Swithin's Day, if it be fair,
> For forty days it will rain no more.

Swithin's Day is named after a 9th-century bishop of Winchester, once the capital of England. It falls on July 15th each year. Is the forecast correct? It is certainly true that the pattern of weather in the middle of July in England often lasts for some time afterwards. Bear in mind that *forty days* in proverbs means simply *a long time*. Other long-range predictions are more obviously true:

> January brings the snow,
> Makes our feet and fingers glow.
> February brings the rain,
> Thaws the frozen lake again.
> March brings breezes sharp and chill,
> Shakes the dancing daffodil …

Of course, until instruments existed for accurately recording temperature and atmospheric pressure, the written records were along the lines of 'warmer and wetter than yesterday'. In 1592, an Italian named Galileo invented a **thermometer** that could record temperature accurately. By the 17th century, people were making temperature observations that led to more accurate *repetition* forecasting in many places. However, it was still not possible to predict tomorrow's weather with any accuracy. In 1643, Galileo's pupil, Torricelli, invented the **barometer** and measured atmospheric pressure. A German called Otto von Guericke started to use the instrument for weather forecasting in 1672. Anyone who has ever owned a barometer knows the principle. When the atmospheric pressure is falling, there is, generally speaking, bad weather on the way, and vice versa. It was not long before weather lore appeared to predict the weather from the barometer, or 'glass', as it was often called:

> When the glass falls low,
> Stand by for a blow;
> When it slowly rises high,
> Light sails you may fly.

By the middle of the 18th century, therefore, people with a thermometer and a barometer could predict their local weather for the next 12 hours with some accuracy. They could also say where the weather was going to, since it was widely known that the wind carried the weather from one location to another. However, accurate observations in Town A were irrelevant to people in Town B, downwind of A, unless the information could be rapidly conveyed to them. It was not until the widespread use of the telegraph in the 1850s that information about weather could be transmitted across countries like the United States and Britain.

So, by the beginning of the 20th century, weather could be accurately recorded in one place, at least in terms of temperature and pressure, and that data could be transmitted quickly to another place. The age of *there today, here tomorrow* forecasting had arrived.

Forecasting Today – Science or Art?

There are two stages to modern weather forecasting. The first stage is collecting information. The second stage is predicting changes in weather, based on the information collected. The first stage is a very well-developed science. To some extent, the second stage is still an art.

There are many ways that information is collected nowadays about weather conditions. The most common are weather ships and weather buoys at sea, weather stations – both manned and automated – on land, weather balloons in the air and weather satellites above the atmosphere. Together, these collection devices give us a clear picture of what is happening now all over the world.

Collection devices at sea and on the land measure a number of aspects of weather. These include air pressure, temperature, wind direction and speed, cloud cover and precipitation, which is the amount of rain or snow that has fallen recently.
Barometers measure pressure.
Thermometers measure temperature.
A simple **weather vane** can be used to measure wind direction. However, a weather vane cannot measure speed. For this, we need an anemometer. A simple **anemometer** is four cups on the ends of weather vane arms. The cups catch the wind and spin. The device spins faster as the speed of the wind increases, and the revolutions are counted to measure the wind speed.
A **pie chart** is used to record cloud cover. Nowadays, a computer can determine the amount of cloud, but in the past it was necessary for someone to take readings every hour and record them on a pie chart. The chart has four sections. If the observer sees broken cloud, for example, he colours in three of the sections. Precipitation is measured with a **rain gauge**. This is simply a tube that is open at the top with a scale on the side. Readings are taken regularly, usually every 24 hours, and the tube is emptied.
All these observations can be recorded on a weather map with standardized symbols that forecasters all around the world can read.

Observations at ground level are only half of the story when it comes to forecasting weather. Weather balloons, technically **radiosondes**, measure temperature, pressure and humidity, which is the amount of moisture in the atmosphere. Together, these measurements tell forecasters about weather fronts, which were discovered during World War I. While armies were fighting at the front in France, a Norwegian meteorologist, Vilhelm Bjerknes, discovered that air masses were fighting in the atmosphere. Nowadays, weather forecasters talk about warm fronts and cold fronts. A warm front has warm moist air behind it. A cold front has cold air behind it. When a warm front meets a cold front, the warm air rises and forms clouds that produce rain. Fronts are shown on weather maps as arcs, with either red semicircles for a warm front or blue triangles for a cold front. By measuring temperature, pressure and humidity, weather balloons enable forecasters to plot fronts.

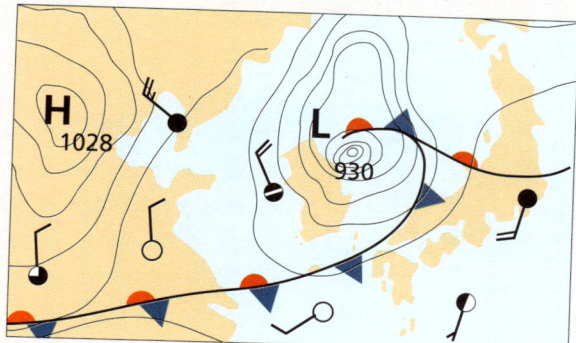

The radiosondes are tracked from the ground, which gives a measurement for wind speed at the altitude of the balloon. Altitude, or height above ground level, is important, because weather forecasters now know that there is a fast-moving wind between seven and ten kilometres above the ground, which is called the jet stream. This wind carries weather systems around the Earth. In the 1930s, radiosondes first recorded the wind and, in 1939, a German meteorologist, Seilkopf, named it *Strahlströmung*, which means 'jet stream'. British and American pilots in World War II noticed that they could fly eastwards at altitudes of 7.5 kilometres much more quickly than westwards.

The final, and most recent, data-collection instrument is the **satellite**. Since 1960, satellites have sent photographs down to Earth that show weather systems across the globe. Nowadays, satellites cover the whole globe and send pictures every 30 minutes.

The World Meteorological Organization (WMO) has 150 member countries that receive data from 10,000 land stations, 7,000 ships and buoys, hundreds of balloons and several satellites. Weather centres in Moscow, Washington, DC, and Melbourne, Australia, assemble the data and make regional forecasts that they send to members of the WMO. From these regional forecasts, national and local forecasts can be made.

Once the data for current weather around the world has been collected and plotted on a weather map, forecasters try to predict what will happen in the future. In principle, the job is quite simple. If it is raining in Town A a hundred miles to the west of Town B, the wind is westerly and has a speed of ten miles an hour, it will be raining in Town B in ten hours. In practice, things are much more complicated. Computers model weather systems in order to predict how they will move, but forecasting is still not an exact science. Firstly, local conditions have an enormous effect on weather in a particular location, and these conditions cannot be included in the models. Secondly, the models themselves are not perfect representations of the atmosphere. Forecasters will sometimes prefer to make a judgement based on their experience rather than on the prediction from the model. One example shows the problem. Forecasters can predict with high accuracy where clouds will form, but they cannot be sure that a particular cloud formation will produce precipitation. There is a theory that droplets form on tiny ice crystals in the cloud, but low-altitude clouds produce rain, too, and they do not contain ice crystals. Modern high-speed computers can do a million calculations a minute, but even at this speed, they cannot take into account all the possible variables in the time available.

Weather forecasting is now extremely accurate, especially for the next five days. However, meteorologists still do not fully understand what causes local weather conditions, and even modern computers cannot do all the necessary calculations fast enough to predict perfectly. As a weather forecaster once said, 'With my computer, I can predict tomorrow's weather with 100 per cent accuracy, but it will take me one week.'

Petroleum

INTRODUCTION

*Petroleum, or **oil**, as it is commonly called, is a naturally occurring hydrocarbon (a chemical compound containing only hydrogen and carbon). It is found on or below the surface of the Earth.*

Scientists have debated the origins of petroleum for many years. However, it is now widely accepted that oil was formed in prehistoric times from organic substances. Petroleum is used as a fuel in vehicle engines. It is also used to generate electricity. In addition, petroleum is an important raw material, or basic substance, in several chemical industries, including the manufacture of plastics, textiles and medicines.

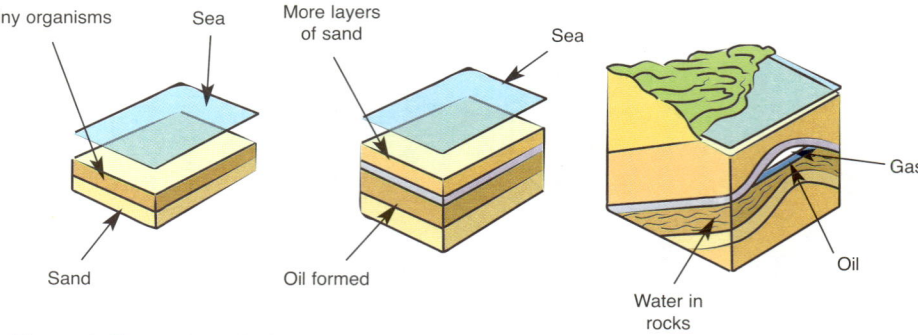

Figure 1: *Formation of oil*

FORMATION

Although petroleum may be found on the surface of the Earth in some parts of the world, it was formed deep beneath the surface. At a time when the Earth was largely covered by water, the sea was filled with tiny organisms. These creatures died, sank to the seabed and were covered in fine sand. As more organisms were deposited on top, the pressure increased and the organic remains were transformed, or changed, into petroleum and natural gas. There was saltwater in the gaps between the rocks, but petroleum has a lower density so it flowed upwards. However, in most cases, it became trapped beneath an impermeable layer, a layer that did not let liquid through. If a hole is drilled through this layer, the petroleum is released and, still under tremendous pressure, it often flows out of the drill hole without any pumping.

HISTORICAL DEVELOPMENT

Petroleum in ancient civilizations

People have known about petroleum for thousands of years because of surface deposits. Five thousand years ago, the Egyptians sealed their pyramids with pitch, which is the sticky remains of natural petroleum. At about the same time, the Sumerians and Babylonians used petroleum to hold their buildings together. Boats along the Euphrates were made with woven reeds and sealed with pitch. The Ancient Chinese used petroleum for heating.

Petroleum products were also used as weapons. The Arabs distilled petroleum from surface deposits to obtain new products. *Distillation* is the process of boiling a liquid then condensing the vapour.

First products from petroleum

When they invaded Spain, the Arabs carried the art of distilling petroleum into Western Europe. By the 1600s, the distillation of petroleum produced lubricants that reduced the friction of turning wheels. It also produced medicines, such as ointments for rubbing on damaged skin.

Exploitation of petroleum

About 200 years ago, the true exploitation of petroleum began. People realized that there was a need for a cheap and convenient source of lighting. In 1852, a Canadian physicist and geologist, Abraham Gessner, obtained a patent for a lamp fuel, which he called *kerosene*. The invention was a small beginning, but it earned Gessner the title 'The Father of Petroleum'.

Scientists began to discover the wide range of products that could be distilled from petroleum. Active exploration for underground oil began.

People had been drilling into the ground for generations to find and extract water. Some people had noticed this water was occasionally contaminated by (mixed with) oil. People realized you could drill for oil as well as water.

Drilling for oil

The first well was dug in Germany in 1857, but the one that caught public attention was drilled near Oil Creek in Pennsylvania in 1859. It hit a reservoir of light oil like kerosene. The invention of the internal combustion engine shortly afterwards ensured a ready market for the main product of the new technology.

In 1908, oil was discovered in Iran, and during the next 40 years, discoveries occurred all over the Middle East, in Iraq, Kuwait and other Gulf states. After the Second World War, the development of the petroleum industry in the region led to massive economic expansion.

FINDING PETROLEUM
Geology and logging

At one time, geologists could not predict the underground structure from the surface appearance. Nowadays, they can identify potential sites for underground oil fields from the geology of the area. Exploratory wells can then be dug to provide further information. In addition, the well can be logged, a process that involves dropping a complex sensor down the exploratory well. However, even with this sophisticated equipment, it remains true that most oil fields are detected from the presence of surface deposits, which result from oil seeping (or moving slowly upwards) from the reservoir.

Wildcat wells

When a seepage was found in the early days, a group of men would clear the area and drill an exploratory well. Small-scale exploration for oil beneath surface deposits is called 'wildcatting' in the oil industry because those pioneer oilmen often had to remove wild cats from the area before they could start to drill.

Size of oil fields

Thousands of oil fields have been discovered in the world, by systematic geologic methods and logging or by wildcatting, but most fields are tiny. The majority of the world's recoverable oil is concentrated in a few gigantic fields. In one area, for example, there are 10,000 oil fields, but just 50 of those account for half the total production of the area.

THE FUTURE

People often say that oil will run out within 50 years. However, that statement is not strictly true. In 50 years' time, there will still be an enormous amount of oil in the ground. However, the question is *Will recovery still be economically viable?* In other words, will it cost less to recover the oil than the value of the oil recovered? It does not matter how much oil is under the ground if it is irrecoverable at an economic rate.

Gessner's kerosene lamp

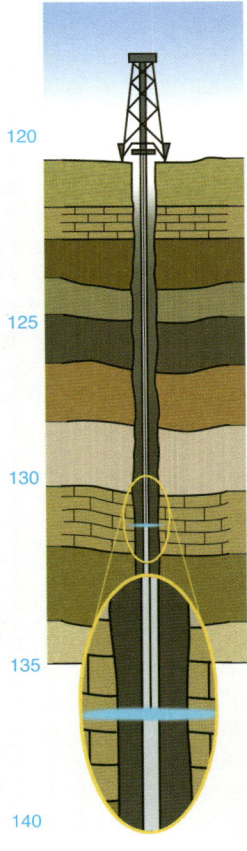

Figure 2: *Well-logging*

ENHANCED RECOVERY
Why do we need it?

When an oil field is first discovered, the oil in the reservoir (underground lake) usually flows from the wells under its own pressure. However, the pressure quickly drops as the oil flows and, after only a small amount of the reserves has been extracted, the remaining reserves are irrecoverable using the field's own energy, which means they cannot be extracted from the field. This point can be reached when only three or four per cent of the reserves have been extracted, but will certainly arrive before a quarter of the field has been tapped. Methods have been developed, therefore, to enhance the recovery – in other words, to improve it. Using these methods, production can be increased to around a third of the total reserves.

Is it worth doing?

Enhanced oil recovery is basically the process of adding energy to raise the pressure in the field. Inevitably, adding energy adds cost, and, eventually, enhanced methods become unviable. In other words, it costs more to produce the oil than the value of the oil produced.

How does enhanced recovery work?

In a fully developed oil field, wells are drilled in many locations, and the distance between two wells may be anything up to 600 metres. Extra wells can be drilled between the extracting wells. These extra wells can receive water or steam injections instead of producing oil.

Water injection

If water is injected into or pumped down the extra wells, the pressure in the reservoir as a whole can be maintained. It can even be increased so the oil flows more quickly out of the extraction wells.

Oil floats on water; therefore, the water injection method can actually raise the oil in the well and further improve recovery efficiency. This method can result in up to 60 per cent more oil being recovered. The method was probably discovered by accident in the late 19th century, when water flooded into an oil reservoir.

Steam injection

Oil fields in different parts of the world contain different kinds of oil. Some oil is very thin, some is very viscous, or thick. Obviously, thin oil flows easily under its own pressure, but viscous oil does not. If steam is injected into extra wells, however, it produces two effects. Firstly, it raises the pressure in the reservoir and keeps the oil flowing. Secondly, the heat in the steam reduces the viscosity, which means that the oil flows more quickly.

This method is quite new and still in development, but it is being used experimentally in Venezuela and in Canada. If it proves successful, we will be able to rely

PRODUCTION VOLUME AND RESERVES

Table 1: *Major oil-producing countries*

Rank	Country	Thousand million barrels p.a.
1	Saudi Arabia	3.12
2	USA	2.80
3	Former USSR	2.60
4	Iran	1.33
5	Mexico	1.11
6	China	1.09
7	Venezuela	1.07
8	Norway	1.02
9	UK	0.95
10	UAE	0.82
11	Canada	0.81
12	Kuwait	0.76

Table 2: *Major oil reserves*

Rank	Country	Thousand million barrels
1	Saudi Arabia	262
2	Iraq	98
3	Kuwait	97
4	UAE	93
5	Iran	88
6	Venezuela	68
7	Former USSR	57
8	Mexico	52
9	Libya	29
10	USA	27
11	China	24
12	Nigeria	21

Refining

Crude oil is the form of petroleum that is found on the surface or in underground reservoirs. In this form, it cannot be used for many purposes. However, crude oil can be refined into many different products, including petrol, asphalt and lubricants. *Refining* is the process of extracting from the crude or original material the useful substances that it contains.

The refining process that is used is called *fractional distillation*. The name comes from the way that the fractions (or parts) that make up crude oil can be recovered by heating. As the crude oil is heated, particular fractions vaporize, or turn into a gas, leaving the rest in liquid form. The vapour can be returned to a liquid by distillation, which involves cooling the gas.

In oil refining, petrol vaporizes out of the crude oil first, while all the rest of the oil is still liquid. Kerosene, which is the fuel used nowadays in jet engines, is next. The last substance to be vaporized is bitumen, which forms the basis of asphalt for making roads.

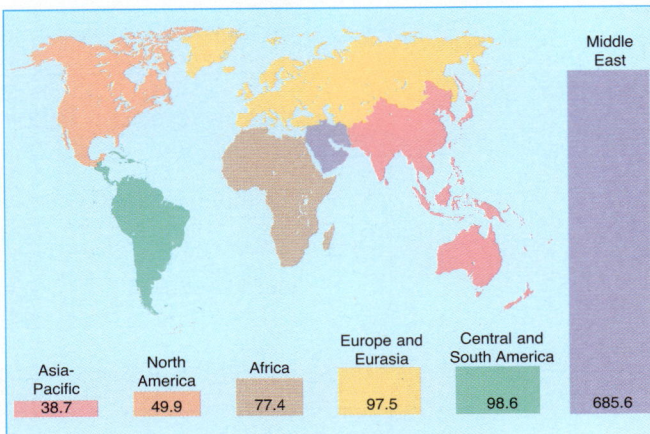

Figure 3: *Oil reserves by continent*

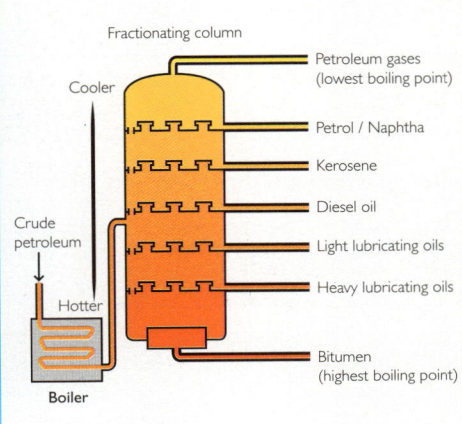

Figure 4: *Products from petroleum*

THEME 1 — Education — Teaching and Learning — Grammar Skills

Read the sentences. Circle the correct word in each case.

1	What	the aim of the lesson was? **was the aim of the lesson?**	
2	How	did the teacher the teacher did	assess Ibrahim's language skills?
3	Which What	one of the learning aims	was achieved?
4	Which What	type of lesson was it –	Presentation, Practice or Production?
5	How many of the world's population	did learn not did not learn	to read or write at school?
6	Professor Hatem Al Hamza	will is going to	talk about language acquisition at 3 p.m. in room 11.
7	Many adults	will are going to	fail to learn a foreign language.
8	After the age of six, one	isn't going to won't	be able to acquire a language.
9	Scientists	won't aren't going to	be able to provide proof of a L.A.D.
10	Look! Zeineb	is going to will	finish the assessment test first!
11	Teaching	doesn't always lead	to learn. to learning.
12	To plan Planning	lessons effectively	helps teachers to achieve learning aims.
13	If you want to pass the exam it will mean	studying to study	hard.
14	The professors dislike students	not arriving not to arrive	on time.
15	Before	to start starting	the course, see Dr. Jarboa.
16	When you read a text you should	to skim skim	for the main idea.
17	Deductive learners	ought ought to	learn the rules.
18	You	shouldn't shouldn't to	look at the answers first!
19	Lessons	must to must	have clear learning aims.
20	Students	don't have to haven't to	have a teacher, they can study by distance.

A Look at Table 1.

1 Match question forms a-h with noun phrases i-viii.

a What/Which	e Why	i a person	v a reason
b Who	f How	ii a place	vi the price/quantity
c Where	g How long	iii a time	vii a period of time
d When	h How many/much	iv the way	viii a thing/object

2 Circle the correct option to make each statement correct.
   a *Which / What* is used when we have a few choices.
   b *Which / What* is used when we have a greater number of choices.
   c In subject questions *we use / don't use* do, does or did.
   d In object questions we use do, does or did between the question word and the *subject / object*.

3 Complete Table 1 with the question forms in Exercise 1.

Table 1: *Question forms*

_____ remembered to revise for the exam this weekend?	Not me, I forgot!
_____ _____ you study English last year?	By distance training.
_____ types of lesson ___ you prefer teaching?	Practice or Production ones.
_____ skills _____ the learners improve in your lesson?	Their writing skills.
_____ _____ Yasmin find time to memorize all those words?	Today; she got up at 5 a.m.!
_____ you distinguish fact from opinion?	By reading the text carefully.

B Look at Table 2.

1 Circle the correct option for the rules about using *will/going to,*
   a We use going to / will:
      • to talk about decisions already made, plans or intentions.
      • to make predictions when we have evidence for them.
   b We use going to / will:
      • to make predictions about things we think, believe or know about the future.
      • for spontaneous decisions.

2 Complete Table 2 with the correct form of the verb.

Table 2: Will/going to

Look at your grades, Ali,	you _____ (not pass) the course	if you dont study h arder!
When children make grammar mistakes in L1	their mothers _____ _____ (not correct)	them.
Oh no! The library's shut!	I _____ (go) to the Internet cafe	instead.
As she's an inductive learner	she _____ (do)	exercise A2.
Good morning class! Today	we _____ (learn) about	the L.A.D.

C Look at Table 3.

1 Match modal verbs a-c and meanings i-iii
   a have to   i for very strong obligation, often giving our personal feelings.
   b must   ii for advising, e.g., *It's a good idea* or *It's the right thing to do.*
   c should/ought to   iii for obligation or duty, often to talk about rules, regulations or laws.

2 Complete Table 3 with the correct modal verb.

Table 3: *Modal verbs of advice* – should/ought to, have to, must.

Students on distance learning courses	_____	submit work by e-mail.
Learners	_____	find out their preferred learning style.
You	_____	not use a calculator in the exam.
I	_____	assess what my students learned today.

D Look at Table 4.

Here are some rules about the gerund/ ~*ing* form. Read them and choose the correct option in Table 4.
We use the gerund/ ~*ing* form:
- as the subject, object or complement of the verb.
- after certain verbs and expressions:
  - *consider, avoid, miss, finish, go, stop, suggest, practise.*
  - verbs of *like* and *dislike*, e.g., *like, love, dislike, mind, hate, can't stand.*
  - *It's no use …, There's no point in …*
- after prepositions.

Note the difference in meaning between *remember doing* and *remember to do, forget doing* and *forget to do*.

Table 4: *Gerunds/~*ing *forms*

Studying / To study	rules is really important	for deductive learners.
Some students find	*revising / to revise*	difficult without proper organization.
Have you considered	*to read / reading through*	the text quickly first?
It's a good idea	to read the text thoroughly before	*to attempt / attempting* the multiple choice questions.
Zohra dislikes	*memorizing / to memorize*	new words, she likes using them!
Good teaching	is about	*to help / helping* people to learn.

THEME 2 — Daily Life — Types of People — Grammar Skills

Read the sentences. Circle the correct word in each case.

#			
1	The twins	live / **have lived** (circled)	apart since birth.
2	Professor Bouchard	threw / has thrown	doubt on the theory in 1980.
3	The university	is never / has never	experimented on animals.
4	Osman	has lived / is living	here for ten years.
5	Drive carefully –	it has	rained. / been raining.
6	Scientists	are / have been	studying that for years, but they haven't reached a conclusion yet.
7	His father	was not / didn't	take him to see the baseball game.
8	The research paper	was / was been	published four years ago.
9	The factors involved aren't	thought / thinking	to be purely genetic.
10	People's height is	been affected / affected	by hereditary factors.
11	Those identical twins	didn't bring up / weren't bought up	in the same country.
12	Where	do you look / is looked	for evidence of this effect?
13	The study was based on brothers who	are / were	separated at birth.
14	Some philosophers	was used to / used to	believe that environment affected appearance.
15	Last week he didn't	use to have / have	a moustache.
16	Did you use / Was you used	to have	a phobia of spiders when you were younger?
17	He	usually smokes / used to smoke	20 cigarettes a day but then he quit.
18	Professor Morgan said it was	inlikely / unlikely	to be the case.
19	The experiments	were said to be	unethical. / nonethical.
20	He was totally	irresponsible; / unresponsible;	he forgot to lock the lab!

A Look at Tables 1a and 1b.
  1 Complete Table 1a with the correct form of the verb *work*.
  2 Complete the rules below with present perfect simple, present perfect continuous, or both.
    a We use _____ tenses to talk about:
      – actions or states that started in the past and continue in the present.
      – completed actions or activities that are relevant now, at the moment of speaking.
    b When we have a choice between both tenses we use:
      – the _____ when we want to suggest something is temporary.
      – the _____ to talk about permanence and/or length.
  3 Complete Table 1b

Table 1a: *Present perfect (simple and continuous)*

Subject	Aux(s)	Verb	
I/You/We/They	have	worked there for years.	present perfect simple
He/She/(It)	_____	_____ here since 1999.	
I/You/We/They	_____ been	working here for 3 days.	present perfect continuous
He/She/(It)	has _____	working in Paris.	

Table 1b: *Present perfect simple, present perfect continuous, or both?*

The debate	_____ (go on)	for years.
Professor Morgan	_____ (study)	these twins for some months.
Khaled	_____ (play) chess all day,	but he ___ only ___ (win) one game!
'Science Today'	_____ (interview)	three different experts this week.
They	_____ (clone)	those plants all semester.

B Look at Tables 2a and 2b.
  1 Study the grammar rules below:
    – Passive forms are used when we are more interested in what is/was done than who does/did it. They are common in academic and scientific writing.
    – We form the **present simple passive** with the present simple of the verb *to be* + the past participle.
    – We form the **past simple passive** with the past simple of the verb *to be* + the past participle.
  2 Complete Table 2a with the correct form of the verb *teach*.
  3 Complete Table 2b with the correct forms of the verb in brackets.

Table 2a: *Present/past simple passive*

Subject	Aux.	Past participle	
I	_____	taught.	
You/We/They	_____	_____.	present simple passive
He/She/(It)	_____	_____.	
I	_____	_____.	
You/We/They	_____	_____.	past simple passive
He/She/(It)	_____	_____.	

Table 2b: *Present or past simple passive?*

The way you	_____ (bring up)	affects your likes and dislikes.
The DNA research	_____ (supervise)	by Doctor Bin Hamza last semester.
The effect on peas	_____ (discover)	by Gregor Mendel in the 19th century.
He	_____ (pay)	for his work by the university.
My height	_____ (inherit)	from my mother; she is 1.92 m tall!

C Look at Table 3.
Study the rules below. Then choose the correct verb form to complete Table 3.
- We use *used to* + infinitive to talk about past habits and states that are finished or no longer the case. This structure is more common in spoken than written language.
- *Used to* is not used to talk about what happened in the past.
- The negative form is *did + not + use to +* infinitive
- The question form is *did + subject + use to +* infinitive

Table 3: Used to *for past habits and states*

The students	used to work / worked	hard on the research project last month.
Mohammed	didn't use to smoke / didn't smoke,	but now he smokes about 20 a day!
The Jim twins both	used to work / worked	as a deputy sheriff for three years.
Did you use to see / Did you see	the results	of the experiment I did in May this year?

D Make the words in Table 4 negative with in~, im~, dis~, un~, ir~, il~ mis~ or anti~.

Table 4: *Negative prefixes*

Adjectives	Verbs
___retrievable	___like
___successful	___communicate
___helpful	___inform
___interesting	___trust
___logical	___do
___predictable	___place
___developed	
___moral	
___social	

THEME 3 — Work and Business | Managing People — Grammar Skills

Read the sentences. Circle the correct word in each case.

#			
1	Many employees refused	working / **to work**	unpaid overtime.
2	Most managers admitted	that they had / to have	hiring problems.
3	The consultants warned them not to	signing / sign	the agreement.
4	Senior managers denied	to advertise / that they advertised	vacancies internally first.
5	The report persuaded	us to evaluate / evaluating	our selection procedures.
6	We suggested	using / them to use	different factors for assessments.
7	The staff were accused	of / that	not having worked hard enough.
8	If researchers didn't	ask the right questions	we couldn't give the right answers! / we didn't give the right answers!
9	If you	didn't / hadn't	have to work, you wouldn't worry!
10	If I met the President	I will / I'd	tell him my opinion.
11	Managers	wouldn't / don't	enjoy their jobs if they were paid less.
12	If I was the boss / If I am the boss	I would / I did	hire fewer consultants.
13	My stress levels	wouldn't / didn't	be so high if I worked part-time.
14	Men	felt that presumably / presumably felt that	this was more important.
15	It seems that most workers	supported / to support	these ideas.
16	The results were clear.	Seemingly, the company / The company seemingly	was at fault.
17	Recruiting more managers	possibly isn't / isn't possibly	worthwhile.
18	The factors involved	were	probably not the same. / not the same probably.
19	The Government	changed the policy	last year, apparently. / apparently last year.
20	Presumably / Certainly	the work was easier	because of the number of extra staff.

A Look at Tables 1a and 1b.
  1 Study the rules below:
    - To report what was said, without any extra information, use *say* or *ask*.
    - Some reporting verbs tell you what the speaker's purpose was (*suggest, believe, think, acknowledge, concede, predict, warn, comment,* etc.)
    - There are six patterns for reporting verbs:
      a verb + *to* + infinitive
      b verb + *~ing* form
      c verb + *(that)* + clause
      d verb + object + *(that)* + clause
      e verb + object + *to* + infinitive
      f verb + object + preposition + *~ing* form
  2 Complete Table 1a.
  3 Which pattern do the verbs in the table belong to?
  4 Look at Table 1b and report the statements using the correct form of the verb.

Table 1a: *Reporting verbs*

Evidently, workers	_____ (believe)	(that)	job security is of vital importance.
The report	_____ (suggest)	(that)	management and workforce needs are similar.
The faculty head	_____ (think)	(that)	a 'fat cat' view of managers was common.
Managers	_____ (warn)		workers to avoid working overtime
Women	_____ (accuse)		men of avoiding responsibility for the situation.
Men	_____ (admit)	(that)	having a friendly boss wasn't important.
The company	_____ (refuse)		to make an official statement until the New Year.
Public opinion	_____ (persuade)		the government to commission an enquiry.

Table 1b: *Reporting verbs and indirect speech*

Manager: 'I will promote you next year.'	(promise/me)
Consultant: 'You should think carefully about the way you manage your staff.'	(recommend/we)
Boss: 'Don't forget to recognize workers' needs.'	(remind/managers)
Researcher: 'This was the case last year.'	(advise/us)
Boss: 'Nobody has job security at the moment!'	(warn/workers)
Worker: 'It's his fault, he wasn't here yesterday.'	(blame/colleague)

B Look at Table 2a.
  1 Study the rules below:
    - The **second conditional**: *If* + past simple / *would* + infinitive
    - We use the **second conditional** to talk about things which are impossible or unlikely to happen in the future, and their consequences.
    - We can use other modals as well as *would* (e.g., *might, may, could*)
  2 Complete Table 2a with the correct forms of the verbs.
  3 Complete the sentences in Table 2b so they are true for you.

Table 2a: *Second conditionals*

If our staff (want) _____ have a good time,	they (not come) _____ to work!
If we (work) _____ for a boss we respected,	we might (be) _____ happier!
If employees (feel) _____ their work was worthwhile,	they _____ (not mind) doing overtime.
If I _____ (not be) so motivated in my workplace,	I _____ (consider) applying for a new job.
If you _____ (assess) your stress levels right now,	you _____ (find) them very high.
If it _____ (be) my decision,	everyone _____ (receive) a pay rise!

Table 2b: *Second conditionals*

If I really wanted to _____	I _____.
If my English was perfect,	I _____.
If our teacher didn't _____,	we _____.
If the sun wasn't _____,	it _____.
If you weren't here now, _____,	where _____?
If people didn't _____ so much,	the world _____!

C Look at Table 3.

1 Put these adjuncts/adverbials below on the right place on the scale:

possibly   seemingly/it seems (that)   definitely   presumably   perhaps   probably   apparently

certainly   *maybe*

⬅ — ➡

The writer is stating a supposition s/he is sure about   *The writer is making a neutral supposition*   *The writer is stating a supposition s/he is less sure about*

2 Note that the adjuncts/adverbials appear at the beginning of a sentence, preparing the reader for the writer's supposition, but they can occur in more than one position.

3 Can the adjuncts/adverbials be placed in both indicated positions? Tick ✓ or cross ✗

Table 3: *Adjuncts/adverbials of supposition*

Presumably,	this is ( )	due to the fact that women feel that managers don't respect them.
Perhaps	they were not ( )	stating their true preferences.
( ),	the selection procedure was **seemingly**	biased against female managers.
( )	the short list was **definitely**	not what his senior manager had expected.
It seems (that)	the best applicants ( )	had more than two references.
Probably	the only applications received were ( )	from men.
Apparently	the vacancy was ( )	advertised internally.
( )	the recruitment process **possibly**	needs to be re-evaluated.

THEME 4 — Science and Nature — Dealing With the Weather — Grammar Skills

Read the sentences. Circle the correct word in each case.

#			
1	Lightning is	**far more** (circled) / the most	dangerous than thunder.
2	The Ancient Greeks didn't have	as much information as / so much information than	we do.
3	Not as many of / Not as much of	their predictions	were as accurate as those of today.
4	Aristotle was the earliest meteorologist	of / in	all the world.
5	Weather lore is	a little / by far	the least accurate method of weather forecasting.
6	There are	fewer / less	warm fronts this year.
7	That's not	my data, it's	your. / yours.
8	The thermometer was	he / his	invention in the year 1592.
9	Its	record-keeping isn't good	in mine opinion. / in my opinion.
10	Our / Ours	isn't as accurate as	yours is.
11	He's observing / He observes	the cloud formations	at the moment.
12	The cold air masses	had been forming / have been formed	across Asia for days.
13	They	have been measuring / have been measured	the air pressure twice a day since 1960.
14	On the way home, the plane will be	flying / fly	faster, as it's eastwards.
15	They	were collecting / collected data	when they heard thunder.
16	Observations were	making / being made	while they worked.
17	In the 17th century, people	could / can	record the temperature with a thermometer.
18	The WMO	can / can to	make regional forecasts.
19	We	couldn't able to / weren't able to	transmit our data last night.
20	Weather forecasters	couldn't / can't	predict the weather perfectly.

RESOURCES BOOK LEVEL 3A – GRAMMAR SKILLS – THEME 4

A Look at Table 1
1 Match a–e with i–vi.
2 Choose the correct option for the rules below.
   a We use _____ adjectives to compare people or things. (comparative / superlative)
   b We use _____ adjectives to compare someone or something with everyone or everything else in a particular group. (comparative / superlative)
   c To talk about _____ differences we use *much/a lot/far* + comparative adjective. (big / small)
   d To talk about _____ differences we use *a little/a bit/slightly* + comparative adjective. (big / small)
   e We can compare quantity by using *more/the most/less/the least* with _____ nouns or *more/the most/fewer/the fewest* with _____ nouns. (countable / uncountable)
   f After superlatives we use _____ before the names of places or groups of people and _____ in most other cases. (of / in)
3 Compare the similarities and differences between:
   a your country and a neighbouring country.
   b your language and English.
   c your classmates.

Table 1: *Comparative and superlative adjectives and expressions*

a	Double glazing is a lot more …	i	… other rooms.
b	Kitchens don't need as much heating as …	ii	… energy efficient than single glazing.
c	Not as much heat escapes from insulated houses …	iii	… there will be fewer draughts.
d	Bathrooms need the least heat of …	iv	… all the rooms in the home.
e	By far the most energy waste is detected in …	v	… as uninsulated ones.
f	If you insulate your home …	vi	… houses with air conditioning.

B Look at Tables 2a and 2b.
1 Separate the possessive adjectives and pronouns below:

myyourhisitsherourtheirtheirsminehishersyoursitsours

2 Now complete Table 2a.
3 Look at the rules below and complete Table 2b by choosing the correct option.
   • We use possessive adjectives before a noun or noun phrase to show possession.
   • We don't use articles or other determiners (e.g., *this/that*) with possessive adjectives.
   • Possessive pronouns are used without articles or following nouns.

Table 2a: *Possessive pronouns and adjectives*

Subject pronouns	Possessive pronouns	Possessive adjectives
I		
you		
she		
he		
it		
we		
they		

Table 2b: *Possessive pronouns and adjectives*

'Is this *our / ours* barometer, or *theirs / their*?'	'Actually, it's *my / mine*.'
The invention was John's idea,	not *hers / her*.
Its / It's accuracy is due to	*our / ours* hard work.
Yours / Your calculations are not as accurate	as the *ours / ours*.
Theirs / Their roof is as well insulated as	*yours / your* roof.

C Look at Table 3

1 Look at the rules below and complete the table with the correct form of the verbs.
- We form the continuous aspect with *be + ~ing*
- We use the continuous aspect to:
    a emphasize that an action is repeated.
    b describe an action in progress at a particular time.
    c indicate that the speaker sees the situation as ongoing and temporary.
    d emphasize that something continues for a period of time.
- Remember that some verbs cannot normally be used in the continuous aspect (e.g., verbs describing hopes, wishes, likes and dislikes, preferences and beliefs)

2 Which use of the continuous aspect is shown? Complete column 3.

Table 3: *The continuous aspect*

		Which use a–d?
The wind (blow: past continuous) _____	all night.	
Meteorologists (predict: present continuous) _____	weather with greater accuracy these days.	
Computers (forecast: future continuous) _____	the weather by the end of the decade.	
The cold front (move: present perfect continuous) _____	across the country for the last few days.	
The air pressure (rise: past perfect continuous) _____	rapidly before the storm hit the region.	
I (listen: present continuous) _____ to the weather report	at the moment.	

D Look at the rules below and complete Table 4 by choosing the correct option.
- We use *can* to talk about general, or present, ability.
- We use *could* to say that somebody was able to do something whenever they wanted.
- *Can* does not have an infinitive or a past participle, we use *be able to/been able to*.
- To say that you managed to do something on one occasion, we use *was/were able to*.
- After *can/could* we use the infinitive without '*to*'.
- Questions and negatives are made without '*Do*'.

Table 4: Can *and* **could** *for ability*

In those days, scientists *couldn't / can't*	collect data by satellite.
Last week, they *weren't able to / couldn't*	contact the Melbourne weather centre.
The WMO can *assemble / to assemble*	all the necessary data.
A weather vane *can't / couldn't* measure	wind speed.

THEME 5 — The Physical World — Geology — Grammar Skills

Read the sentences. Circle the correct word in each case.

#			
1	The oil flowed more quickly after the water	has / **had**	been injected into the extra wells.
2	The organisms	hadn't / hasn't	always been covered by sand.
3	By the time the Egyptians	sealed / had sealed	their pyramids, the Sumerians found petroleum was useful in building.
4	The Arabs	were / had been	distilling petroleum for years when they invaded Spain.
5	Iranians	had been / had	discovered oil some years before Kuwaitis.
6	Wells are drilled	in / on	many locations.
7	Oil floats	at / on	water.
8	Steam injection is still in development	in / at	Canada.
9	The wildcat wells are found	at / in	the North.
10	Diesel oil is seen in the diagram	below / at	the kerosene.
11	People used to think	the gold / gold	was from volcanoes.
12	There were	a gold rush / gold rushes	in Australia and the States.
13	The rock and earth above	a vein / vein	of gold was dug away first.
14	It is	a very / very	good conductor of heat and electricity.
15	Battery / The battery	conductors for cell phones	are likely to be made of gold.
16	Venezuela	will have been relied on / will be rely on	for extra oil by the end of the century.
17	A quarter of the field will have	been / being	tapped before this point is reached.
18	The pressure can	maintain / be maintained	if water is pumped into them.
19	Electricity will	been generated / be generated	every second it is switched on.
20	Petroleum products	were used / been used	as weapons thousands of years ago.

A Look at the rules below. Complete Table 1 with the correct form of the verbs.

The **past perfect simple** (subject + *had* + past participle) is used to talk about:
- actions that took place before another action or state in the past.
- situations or states that existed before another action or situation in the past.

The **past perfect continuous** (subject + *had* + *been* + *~ing* form verb) is used to talk about:
- actions or situations that started in the past and continued until another point in the past.
- the duration of the action, emphasizing it.
- past situations or repeated actions which explain another present/past action or situation.

Table 1: *Past perfect (simple and continuous)*

A gold rush started in California after Sutter	(find: pps) _____ gold in the late 1840s.
Gold (extract: pps passive) _____ by panning before	underground mines were dug in the 1860s.
When the first Chinese goldminers arrived in 1853	Australians (mine: ppc) _____ there for two years.
South Africa (produce: ppc) _____ most of the gold until	cheaper Californian gold became available.
The lakes were panned for gold after the panners	(divert: pps) _____ the river through four lakes.

B Read the explanation below. Then choose the correct option to complete Table 2.
Prepositions/prepositional phrases tell us where something happens, or where something/someone is.

Table 2: *Prepositions of place*

Durban is located	*at / on* the coast.
Lesotho is surrounded *by / with*	South Africa.
The major mines are *in / on*	the North.
Taking metals found *under / below* the ground	is called 'extraction'.
The pyramids are east of the river *on / in*	the southern border.

C Read the rules below. Then look at Table 3.
We use the indefinite article **a/an**:
- to talk about something unspecific.
- to talk about something for the first time.
- to classify things.

We use the definite article **the**:
- when there is only one of something, to talk about something previously mentioned, or in superlative expressions.
- with buildings, rivers, seas and some countries (where the name has a noun, e.g., the United States).
- with an adjective when we are talking about a group of people (e.g., the young, the helpless).

We use the **zero article**:
- to talk about abstract nouns, plural countable & uncountable nouns when we are generalizing.
- with languages and most place names/countries.
- with certain expressions.

1 Complete Table 3 with *the, a, an* or Ø.
2 Which rule is shown?
3 Now complete the *Why?* column with the reason.

RESOURCES BOOK LEVEL 3A – GRAMMAR SKILLS – THEME 5

Table 3: *Articles*

		Why?
The first oil well was dug in 1857 in	Ø / *the* Germany.	country
The majority of *the / a / Ø* world's oil is concentrated in	*the / a* few enormous fields.	
Some people believe that *the / a / an / Ø* oil	will run out in their lifetime	
How often do they drill for *a / an / the / Ø*	exploratory well?	
When *the / a* seepage was found	they used to drill *a / the / Ø* well.	

D Look at Table 4.
   1 Read the following rules:
      • We use the past simple passive (subject + *was/were* + past participle) to talk about completed finished actions and events.
      • We use the present perfect simple passive (subject + *have/has* + *been* + past participle) to talk about completed actions relevant now.
      • We use the future passive (subject + *will* + *be* + past participle) to talk about actions in the future
      • We can use the passive with modal verbs, *used to* and continuous forms.
   2 Complete Table 4 by choosing the correct option. Name the passive tense used.

Table 4: *Passives*

A patent for kerosene	was obtained by / obtains	Gessner in 1852.
The pressure	is been maintained / can be maintained	by water injection.
Water injection extraction	might have been discovered / might have discovered	by accident.
Crude oil	has been refined / has being refined	into thousands of products.
When the crude oil	was heated / would be heated	some parts vaporized.

Transcript

Presenter: Skills in English, Level 3, Part A
Theme 1: Education, Teaching and Learning
Section 1: Listening
Lesson 1: Vocabulary for listening
B   Listen to a short text with the green words. Then complete the text with one of the words in each space.

Voice: What is learning? Scientists define learning as a change of behaviour. But how do we learn? Nobody knows for sure, but there are many theories from psychologists and philosophers. Some say, 'People learn from experience. For example, a baby cries and his mother gives him food. He learns that certain behaviour is useful.' Other people think that we learn by observation. They say, 'We look around at the world. We observe other people. We see how they behave. We copy them.'

Presenter: D   2   Listen and number the words you hear.
Voice:
observe
experience
behave
behaviour
learning
theory
observation

Presenter: **Lesson 2:** Practising listening
B   2   Listen to the introduction. Complete the outline.

Female lecturer: How do we learn? This seems like a simple question, but there is no simple answer. In the next two lectures, we are going to look at theories of learning. This week I'm going to talk about theories from the distant past. Firstly, theories from Ancient Greece. Next, theories from Islamic scholars. Finally, a very famous theory from a Russian scientist, Ivan Pavlov. Next week, I'm going to describe the work of two Americans, Skinner and Watson, in the 20th century.

Presenter: C   Listen to the first part of the lecture.
Female lecturer: So, first, to Ancient Greece. The Greek philosopher Plato – that's P-L-A-T-O – lived from 427 BCE to about 347 BCE. He believed that learning was just memory. We have an experience. Maybe it's good. Maybe it's bad. Maybe we remember. Maybe we forget. If we remember later, that's learning by experience. For example, a child touches a fire and burns himself. He remembers next time and doesn't touch the fire.

Presenter: D   Listen to the rest of the lecture. Copy and complete Table 1.
Female lecturer: Plato's student, Aristotle, lived from 384 BCE to 322 BCE. Aristotle is spelt A-R-I-S-T-O-T-L-E. He believed, like Plato, that we learn by doing things. But he went further. He believed that people learn when they see the cause of things, when they understand why something happens. For example, a child touches a fire and burns himself. Later he touches a match and burns himself. He sees a pattern: hot things burn you. After the child sees the pattern, he does not touch any hot things, including irons and boiling water – things that haven't burnt him in the past.

Next, the Islamic scholars. A lot of Greek learning was lost to the Western World in the 5th century AD. But Islamic philosophers and scientists translated the works of Plato and Aristotle. Scholars like Al Farabi in the 9th century AD, Ibn Sina in the 10th century and Ibn Rushd in the 12th century carried forward Aristotle's ideas. They also added theories of their own. A common theme in Islamic science is that learning comes from studying nature. Nowadays, we call this 'learning by observation'. The child observes another child touching a fire. He sees that the other child is burnt. He does not touch the fire himself.

Finally, to Russia and a very important theory. In the 19th century, a Russian psychologist called Ivan Pavlov – that's P-A-V-L-O-V – started to study dogs. He was not interested in learning. He wanted to know why a dog's mouth produced saliva when it got its food. Saliva is necessary for the correct digestion of the food. But why do dogs produce saliva at the right time? First Pavlov thought it was the smell of the food. He tried an experiment. He sent a person to feed some dogs for several days. The dogs produced saliva. Then he sent the same person at the same time … but with no food. The dogs produced saliva when they saw the person. Pavlov realized that the dogs associated the person with food. Pavlov did another experiment to prove his theory. This experiment has become famous. He gave the dogs some food every few minutes. Every time the dogs started to eat the food, Pavlov rang a bell. After a short time, the dogs produced saliva when they heard the bell, even if there was no food. Pavlov continued to ring the bell but stopped giving food at the same time. Eventually, the dogs stopped producing saliva when they heard the bell.

What is the connection between Pavlov's dogs and human learning? Pavlov's experiment led to a new theory about how we learn. Scientists said that events in our environment can change the way we behave. In other words, we learn to behave in a particular way because of the way people and things behave around us. Pavlov called this process 'conditioning'. Pavlov's theory says a child can become frightened of something without having direct experience and without observing someone else having the experience. So, for example, if a mother sees her child is going to touch a fire, she shouts 'No!' She frightens the child. The child connects the fear and the fire, even though he did not get burnt himself or see anyone else getting burnt.

Presenter: **Lesson 3:** Learning new listening skills
C   3   Listen and check your ideas.
Female lecturer: Plato's student, Aristotle, lived from 384 BCE to 322 BCE. Aristotle is spelt A-R-I-S-T-O-T-L-E. He believed, like Plato, that we learn by doing things. But he went further. He believed that people learn when they see the cause of things, when they understand why

	something happens. For example, a child touches a fire and burns himself. Later he touches a match and burns himself. He sees a pattern: hot things burn you. After the child sees the pattern, he does not touch any hot things, including irons and boiling water – things that haven't burnt him in the past.
Presenter:	**D 2 Listen and check.**
Female lecturer:	He gave the dogs some food every few minutes. Every time the dogs started to eat the food, Pavlov rang a bell. After a short time, the dogs produced saliva when they heard the bell, even if there was no food. Pavlov continued to ring the bell but stopped giving food at the same time. Eventually, the dogs stopped producing saliva when they heard the bell.
Presenter:	**E 2 Listen and check.**
Female lecturer:	What is the connection between Pavlov's dogs and human learning? Pavlov's experiment led to a new theory about how we learn. Scientists said that events in our environment can change the way we behave. Pavlov called this process 'conditioning'. Pavlov's theory says a child can become frightened of something without having direct experience and without observing someone else having the experience.
Presenter:	**Lesson 4: Applying listening skills** **B 2 Listen to the introduction. Make outline notes for the lecture.**
Female lecturer:	This is the second of two lectures on the topic: How do we learn? Last week, we talked about a number of theories through history. Firstly, we heard about the theories of Plato and Aristotle in Ancient Greece. Then we learnt about the theories of the Islamic scholars Al-Farabi, Ibn Sina and Ibn Rushd in the Arab World. Finally, I talked about the psychologist, Pavlov, and his famous experiment in 19th-century Russia. We learnt that philosophers believe we learn by remembering, or by understanding why, or by observing or through conditioning. This week, we are going to look at some theories from the 20th century. Firstly, I am going to talk about the theory of an American called Watson. Then, I will describe the theory of another American called Skinner. His ideas had a big effect on the way people started to teach foreign languages.
Presenter:	**C Listen to the first part of the lecture. What is the main point of this part?**
Female lecturer:	John Watson accepted the ideas of Pavlov. He believed that you could extend them to human beings. He believed that experiences in people's lives changed their behaviour. He said this was much more important than any natural behaviour that people inherited from their parents. Watson conducted a famous experiment in 1919 and 1920. He used a baby called Albert in his experiment. He gave baby Albert a white rat. Albert tried to touch the rat. Watson made a loud noise just behind the baby's ear. Albert started to cry. Every time he tried to touch the rat, Watson made a loud noise and frightened the baby. Every time, the baby started to cry. Soon, Albert cried when the rat appeared. In fact, he cried when he saw anything that looked like a rat – a furry toy or a fur coat. Watson's experiment proved that conditioning worked in people as well as animals.
Presenter:	**D Listen to the second part of the lecture. Connect the pictures and explain the main ideas in this part.**
Female lecturer:	Watson's work was important. However, the work of another American, B.F. Skinner, was much more important in the history of education. Skinner worked in a laboratory in the 1940s. He also knew about the work of Pavlov. Pavlov showed that a new stimulus, like a bell ringing, can make an animal produce existing behaviour, like salivating for food. Skinner thought, 'Can I teach animals to learn new behaviour through conditioning?' First, he did experiments with rats. He taught rats to get through very complicated mazes to find food. They had to push buttons and move levers to open doors. At the end of the maze, they found food. Then Skinner did something amazing. He taught pigeons to play table tennis. How did he do this? He watched the pigeons very closely. Every time they did something like push a table tennis ball with their beaks, he gave them some food. Finally, he conditioned the pigeons to play table tennis to get food.
Presenter:	**E Listen to the third part of the lecture. Number these events in order.**
Female lecturer:	Skinner worked with animals, not people, but he believed that his results could apply to people as well. In particular, he said that conditioning pigeons to play table tennis was like conditioning children to speak their own language. For example, a baby makes a sound when his mother comes in the room. The mother thinks the sound is like the word 'Mummy'. She repeats it. This happens hundreds of times. Finally, the child says 'Mummy' when his mother comes into the room.
Presenter:	**Section 2: Speaking** **Lesson 1: Vocabulary for speaking** **C Read and listen to the text. Complete it with a green word or phrase in each space. Make any necessary changes.**
Voice:	What activities are you looking forward to in this theme? Do you like exercises that involve pairwork? Or do you prefer discussions in small groups? What about a role play, where you take the part of a different person and act out a scene? Everybody has a learning style. Some people don't see the point in crosswords and puzzles, while others learn a lot by working things out in this way. What about you? Some people love research, in the library or on the Internet, while others prefer to be told the important information in a lecture. Which type of person are you? My personal favourite is the project that involves making something. I suppose that's because I'm a kinaesthetic learner.
Presenter:	**Lesson 2: Practising speaking** **A 3 Listen and check.**
Voice:	neat career psychologist screen convert restless gestures layout

Presenter:	**Lesson 3:** Learning new speaking skills		
	A 1 Listen to each pair of words or phrases.		
Voice:	a physical	visual	
	b text	ticks it	
	c screen	scare Ian	
	d rings	ring his	
	e career	crier	
	f the things	the thing is	
	g I can do it.	I can't do it.	
	h That sounds good.	That sound is good.	
	i It provides good support.	It provides good sport.	

Presenter: **B 5 Listen and check.**
Voice:
angina
barge
consign
gen
ginger
glade
goad
insignia
thorough

Presenter: **Lesson 4:** Applying speaking skills
A 2 Listen and check.
Voice:
Column 1
making
name
play
say
they

Column 2
pair
their
there
wear
where

Column 3
assignment
designer
find
require
typing

Column 4
go
know
most
role
so

Column 5
about
allowed
around
out
sound

Column 6
career
clear
engineer
hear
idea

Presenter: **Theme 2: Daily Life, Types of People**
Section 1: Listening
Lesson 1: Vocabulary for listening
B Listen to a short text with the green words. Then complete the text with one of the words in each space. Make any necessary changes.

Voice: Do you sometimes ask yourself: 'Who am I?' If you do, you are normal. Indeed, psychologists say that we ask ourselves this question throughout our lives. The meaning of the question changes as we grow up. Babies ask, 'Who am I? Is this hand part of me, or part of you?' Infants ask, 'Who am I? My parents choose my clothes, my food, my school, my bedtime.' Adolescents ask, 'Who am I? A nice person or a nasty one?' Middle-aged adults ask, 'Who am I? What have I done with my life?' We ask the question because, according to Erik Erikson (see Lesson 4), at every age there is an identity crisis – a conflict or battle between who we are and who we would like to be. At every age we find different answers, because, according to Piaget (see Lesson 2), our brains develop in a predictable way through infancy and adolescence to adulthood.

Presenter: **C 2 Listen and check your ideas.**
Voice:
1 birth
2 infancy
3 childhood
4 adolescence
5 adulthood
6 middle age
7 death

Presenter: **Lesson 2:** Practising listening
B Listen to the introduction. Make a set of outline notes for this week's lecture.
Male lecturer: In these two lectures, we are going to look at two theories of child development. Firstly, this week, I'm going to look at Jean Piaget. That's ET at the end because he was a French speaker. Next week, I'll talk about the life and work of Erik Erikson.
OK, so this week, I'm going to talk about Piaget's life and how he developed his ideas. Then I'm going to explain to you Piaget's four stages of child development.

Presenter: **D 1 Listen to the first part of the lecture.**
Male lecturer: Jean Piaget was born in Switzerland on August 9, 1896. When he was 11 years old, he wrote a scientific essay about a small bird. This was the start of a long career of research and writing that included more than 60 books and hundreds of articles.
After birds, he became interested in shellfish. He published many articles on the subject while he was still at school.
After he left school, he studied natural sciences at the University of Neuchâtel – that's N-E-U-C-H-A-T-E-L. He got his PhD and then left Switzerland to work in a school in France. This was the beginning of his work with children, which continued for the rest of his life. He developed a test for intelligence in five- to eight-year olds, and he became interested in the way that brains develop, or what he called 'the biological explanation of knowledge'. He discovered that children at a certain age could solve problems that children at an earlier age could never solve. He decided to find out more.

In 1921, he returned to Switzerland to become director of studies at an institute in Geneva. He got married two years later, and the couple had three children. This was important in his professional as well as his social life. He studied the development of the three children closely, from infancy to adulthood. During the next 40 years, he held a succession of important posts in universities and research institutes. He died in Geneva on September 16, 1980.

Presenter: D 3 Listen again. Put the notes on Piaget's life, work and ideas together.
[REPEAT OF LESSON 2 EXERCISE D1]

Presenter: E Listen to the second part of the lecture.
Male lecturer: For the whole of his adult life, Piaget kept asking the same question: 'How does knowledge grow?' He had the idea, which was unusual at the time, of actually talking to children and finding out their ideas. For example, there is one story about a conversation with a five-year-old girl. He asked her: 'What makes the wind?'
The child replied: 'The trees.'
'How do you know?'
'I saw them waving their arms.'
'How does that make the wind?'
'Like this. Only they are bigger. And there are lots of trees.'
'What makes the wind on the ocean?'
'It blows there from the land. No. It's the waves …'
Piaget said, 'Children only really understand things that they invent themselves. If we try to teach them something too quickly, we stop them reinventing it themselves.'
In another experiment, Piaget told lots of children the same story. He said, 'Imagine that one boy is washing up after dinner and he breaks two cups. Imagine that another boy asks his mother, 'Can I have some chocolate?' and the mother says, 'No'. Then this boy tries to get the chocolate and he breaks a cup. Which child is naughtier?' Young children always answered, 'The first child, because he broke two cups. The other child only broke one cup.' Older children said, 'The second child, because he was doing something naughty when he broke the cup. The first child was trying to be helpful.' This shows that ideas of right and wrong change as children grow up.
Piaget decided, after many years, that knowledge grows in a predictable way, from simple ideas to more complex ones. He concluded that the brain of an infant is different from the brain of a child, and different from the brain of an adolescent or an adult. Piaget's work has influenced people all over the world in many fields, including psychology, sociology and education. His theories of child development are still the basis of most thinking in this area.
So what did Piaget actually discover? He found that there are four major stages of development, although each of these stages has many subdivisions.

Presenter: F Listen to the third part of the lecture.
Male lecturer: The first stage lasts from birth up to about 18 months or two years. He called this stage the sensorimotor stage, that's S-E-N-S-O-R-I-M-O-T-O-R. Babies do not know how things will react, and so they are always experimenting – shaking things, putting things in their mouths, throwing. They are learning by experience. We sometimes call this kind of learning trial and error.
The second stage lasts from 18 to 24 months to 7 years. Piaget called this stage pre-operational. Pre means before, so this is before operational thought. In this stage, children learn to speak. They can pretend and they can understand past and future. However, they cannot understand cause-and-effect. In other words, they cannot understand 'if I do this, this will happen'.
The third stage is from 7 to 12 years. Piaget called this the stage of concrete operational thought. Concrete, spelt C-O-N-C-R-E-T-E, in this case, means real, not abstract. At this stage, children can understand that real things stay the same, even if you move them around. For example, a litre of water is a litre of water in a small bottle or a big bottle.
The final stage of child development happens after about 12 years old. Piaget called this the stage of formal operational thought. Formal in this case means not real, but abstract. At this stage, children can understand algebra – for example, a + b = c, and they can understand hypotheses and abstract ideas like fairness and justice.
So, to sum up, Piaget believed that all children go through these four stages more or less at the same age. Although some people today criticize his ideas, he is still widely regarded as the greatest developmental psychologist of the 20th century. Einstein called his discovery of developmental stages 'so simple that only a genius could have thought of it.'
OK. Next week, Erik Erikson and some more ideas on child development.

Presenter: Lesson 3: Learning new listening skills
B 3 Listen and check your ideas.
Voice: a cause and effect
b in other words
c learning by experience
d life and work
e more or less
f past and future
g professional and social
h right and wrong
i so to sum up
j trial and error
k all over the world
l the rest of his life

Presenter: Lesson 4: Applying new listening skills
A 2 Listen and check your ideas.
Voice: a career
b research
c explanation
d knowledge
e infancy
f adulthood
g professional
h social
i experience
j effect
k algebra
l react
m error
n trial
o theory

Presenter:	**B You are going to hear the second lecture about child development. Listen to the introduction. Make a set of outline notes.**
Male lecturer:	Last week, we talked about the work of Jean Piaget on child development. This week, we are going to look at the life and work of another famous person in this field, Erik Erikson – that's E-R-I-K E-R-I-K-S-O-N. First I'm going to tell you a little about his life, because it is possible that his life influenced his work. Then I'm going to describe his theories of child development.
Presenter:	**C Listen to the first part of the lecture.**
Male lecturer:	Erikson was born in Germany on June 15th, 1902. There is no record of the name of his real father. In 1905, when Erik was three, his mother married Erik's doctor, Theodor Homberger – that's H-O-M-B-E-R-G-E-R. So he grew up as Erik Homberger.
Erikson left school in about 1920. He became an artist and then a teacher. Then he studied child psychology in Austria. During this time he got married. He and his wife emigrated to the United States in 1933. He taught at Yale and Harvard, on the East Coast. In 1939, he moved to California, on the West Coast, to teach at the university at Berkeley. He began to study groups of Native American children. He studied the way they developed the values of their parents.
Also in 1939, Erik Homberger became an American citizen and changed his family name to Erikson. There is an interesting story about this. Erik never knew his real father, but at some point he became aware that his real name was not Homberger. His mother refused to give him any information about his real father. For some reason, Erikson started to believe that he was the son of a royal prince from Denmark. Is that why he gave himself a Danish family name? And did this confusion about his own identity lead to Erik's interest in identity in children?
Erikson moved back to the East Coast of the United States in 1950 and continued working and teaching there until he retired in 1970. He died on May 12th, 1994.
Presenter:	**D Listen to the second part of the lecture.**
Male lecturer:	Erikson published his first book in 1950. It was called *Childhood and Society*. The book is still widely read in the field of psychoanalysis. In this book, Erikson developed his theory of the identity crisis. This is the idea that a child must find its own identity as it moves through various stages of development. It is clear that Erikson did not find his full identity. Even the simplest personal questions seemed to cause a problem for him. There are many stories about this. For example, if someone asked Erikson 'How are you?' he often turned to his wife and said, 'Well, Joan. How are we?' But perhaps the most surprising story is about Erikson and food. If someone gave Erikson some food that he wasn't expecting, he sometimes turned to his wife and asked, 'Do I want this, Joan?'
Presenter:	**E Listen to the third part of the lecture. Copy and complete the table of Erikson's stages of development.**
Male lecturer:	What about his work and ideas? Erikson identified eight stages of development, through childhood and adult life. We are only going to look at the first five stages, because these lectures are about child development, not adult development. At each stage, Erikson said that there is a conflict, a battle, a war, with a good result and a bad result.
The first stage lasts for the first one or two years of life. It is the stage of trust versus mistrust. An infant learns to trust his or her parents and adults in general – or learns that adults are not to be trusted. Trust versus mistrust.
The second stage is from about two years to about four years. It is the stage of self-confidence versus shame. A young child learns to be confident in his ability to do things by himself – or he learns to be ashamed of his failure to do things. Unfortunately for parents, the confident child is also developing willpower, and often refuses to obey. This is difficult for the parents but is part of the child's social development. So the second stage is self-confidence versus shame.
The third stage is from about four to entry into school at five or six. It is the stage of initiative versus guilt. Perhaps those words are new to you. Initiative is spelt I-N-I-T-I-A-T-I-V-E, and it means doing something yourself, without being told to do it. Guilt – G-U-I-L-T – means feeling bad about something you have done wrong. At this stage, the child learns to take initiative, to cooperate with other children, to lead and to follow. The child also learns to imagine and to pretend. This is the wonderful period of make-believe. So, initiative is the good result. Or the child feels guilty and refuses to take part in games, does not play with other children and does not develop play skills or imagination. So this stage is initiative versus guilt.
The fourth stage occurs during the early years of schooling. It is the stage of structured play versus inferiority. Structured play means playing team games with other children. Inferiority – I-N-F-E-R-I-O-R-I-T-Y – means feeling that you are not as good as other children. The child learns to play structured games that involve teamwork. The child also learns self-discipline and manages his or her own homework. A child who has come through stages 1, 2 and 3 successfully will have little difficulty with this stage – he will trust adults and work with initiative. However, the child who has had problems at earlier stages will fail at this stage, too. He will mistrust adults and not take charge of his own life. He will feel shame, guilt and inferiority.
The fifth stage is the stage of adolescence, from 13 or 14 to about 20. It is the stage of identity – of knowing who you are – versus diffusion – that's D-I-F-F-U-S-I-O-N – as Erikson calls it – not knowing who you are. The successful adolescent learns self-confidence rather than self-consciousness, which means being embarrassed about the way you look, the way you speak, the way you dress, etc.
Erikson believed that there are three more stages that occur in adulthood. As we are talking about child development, I am not going to discuss those here. Erikson's theory is that a child needs to learn to socialise – to become part of the society he or she lives in. The job of a parent and a teacher is to help the child to move from being helpless and centred on him or herself, to being a part of society, but also to be an independent thinker.
Presenter:	**F These statements are true or probably true. Listen to the lecture again and find evidence.**
[REPEAT OF LESSON 4 EXERCISES B, C, D AND E]

Presenter:	**Section 2: Speaking** **Lesson 1:** **Vocabulary for speaking** **C 2 Listen and check your answers.**
Voice:	Imagine that you are offered two jobs. Both jobs are interesting. The money is good in both cases. How would you choose between them? How would you decide which job to take? Mary Orwell had this problem. She made a decision quite quickly. She thought about the two alternatives for a few days and then chose one. She is not sure now that this was the best decision, but she is not unhappy about it. She has no regrets at all. 'There is only one thing worse than a bad decision,' she says, 'and that is no decision at all.' Mary's friend, Fleur Arnold, had the same problem, but she behaved in a different way. She thought about the alternatives for a long time, getting more and more information about each job. Finally, she made up her mind. She didn't phone the company, though. She waited for a few more days … and changed her mind. She still didn't accept the job, and finally she changed her mind again and chose the first job. However, she was not happy with her decision. 'I think the other job was better,' she says now.
Presenter:	**Lesson 2:** **Practising speaking** **A 2 Listen and check your ideas.**
Mary:	Hi, Fleur. Do you want a coffee?
Fleur:	I'm not sure.
Mary:	Go on. I'm having one.
Fleur:	OK. I'll have one then.
Mary:	What kind do you want? Cappuccino, latte, americano, espresso …
Fleur:	Stop! Too many choices!
Mary:	What do you mean? Choice is good. I love having lots of choices.
Fleur:	I don't. The more choices I have, the harder it is to make a decision.
Presenter:	**C Listen to the second part of the conversation between Mary and Fleur. Complete this summary of the article.**
Mary:	That's a coincidence.
Fleur:	What is?
Mary:	You said you find it hard to make decisions. I read a really interesting article about decision-making the other day.
Fleur:	Great. Perhaps it can help me. What did it say?
Mary:	Well, apparently, there are two kinds of people, maximizers and satisficers.
Fleur:	You mean satisfiers?
Mary:	No, I'm sure it said satisficers.
Fleur:	Oh, OK.
Mary:	It seems that maximizers are always unhappy with their decisions.
Fleur:	Just like me. But why?
Mary:	Because they always think there was a better alternative.
Fleur:	That does sound like me. And what about satisfiers?
Mary:	Ficers.
Fleur:	Whatever.
Mary:	Well, as I understand it, satisficers make decisions easily because they just want something that is good enough. They are happier in their daily life because they don't regret decisions.
Fleur:	That's fascinating.
Presenter:	**D Listen to the final part of the conversation. Answer the questions.**
Fleur:	Who said all this?
Mary:	I can't remember.
Fleur:	Well, where did you read about it?
Mary:	I don't know. Some newspaper.
Fleur:	So which book does all this appear in?
Mary:	I've no idea.
Fleur:	Oh, Mary! You're hopeless. When you read something interesting, you must make a note of names and publications and so on.
Mary:	Sorry. I'll get the coffee.
Fleur:	Hang on! I haven't decided yet.
Presenter:	**Lesson 3:** **Learning new speaking skills** **A 2 Listen and check your ideas.**
Voice:	behave behaviour believe belief choose choice decide decision maximize maximum produce product regret regret research research satisfy satisfaction solve solution
Presenter:	**B 2 Listen and check your ideas.**
Voice:	a In 1947, an American economist and social scientist called Herbert Simon coined these terms in his book *Administrative Behavior*. b He claimed that there are two kinds of decision maker. Maximizers cannot make decisions easily because there are often good alternatives. c Satisficers, on the other hand, make up their minds quite quickly because they are just looking for something that satisfies their needs. d Does it matter if you are a maximizer or a satisficer? According to Simon, it does. His research showed that people who are maximizers are often dissatisfied with life, while satisficers are not.
Presenter:	**Lesson 4:** **Applying new speaking skills** **A 3 Listen and check your ideas.**
Voice:	a There are often a number of alternatives. b You are already in a lot of trouble. c What an awful old umbrella! d We all agree about the exam answers. e I don't know if I'll ever ask you again.
Presenter:	**Theme 3: Work and Business, Managing People** **Section 1: Listening** **Lesson 1:** **Vocabulary for listening** **A 3 Listen and check your answers.**
Voice:	We often use equations in business. For example, the price of something in a shop usually equals the cost to make it plus some profit for the company. We can write this as an equation: cost + profit = price. Both sides of an equation must be the same. In other words, they must balance. So if the cost is $20 and the profit is $2, the price must be $22. What happens if the cost increases? We can use our equation to make sure the profit stays the same. If the previous cost was $20 and the current cost is $22, then the new price must be $24.

Presenter: **B 3 Listen and check your answers.**
Voice: Equation 1: salary per hour x working hours per week = total salary per week
Example: $10 x 48 hours = $480

Equation 2: working hours per day - rest breaks = total working hours per day
Example: 8 hours - 1.5 hours = 6.5 hours

Equation 3: managers + workers = employees
Example: 5 managers + 100 workers = 105 employees

Presenter: **C 2 Listen to each sentence. What form of the word do you hear? What does the word mean in this situation?**
Voice:
a This is Mr Jones. He is the production manager.
b Good morning, Mr. Jones. What do you actually produce here?
c This is the industrial part of the city. All the factories are here.
d The workers have started to work as a team. They are producing a lot more now.
e We all have a number of needs. We need food and drink and love, for example.

Presenter: **D 2 Listen and check your ideas.**
Voice: balance
current
equal
equation
increase
previous
employee
industrial
produce
production
working

Presenter: **Lesson 2: Practising listening**
C Listen to the introduction.
Female lecturer: This week and next week, I am going to talk about ideas in the field of Industrial Psychology. We know what psychology means – it is the study of how the brain works, of how people think. So what is Industrial Psychology? It is the study of the way people think about work and the effects of working conditions on productivity. Productivity is the amount of work that a person does in one time period, say one day. So for example, if one worker makes five items in one day and another worker makes six items, the second worker has a higher productivity than the first worker. This week, I'm going to talk about the experiment that started Industrial Psychology and the conclusions that the researcher, Elton Mayo, reached about the results. Next week, I'm going to describe the theories of two writers in this field, Maslow and Herzberg.

Presenter: **D 2 Listen to the first part of the lecture. Follow the suggestions in the Skills Check.**
Female lecturer: It all started with a series of experiments at a factory in Chicago in the USA. The factory was called the Hawthorne Works. The experiments were carried out by Elton Mayo. He was an Australian, born on the 26th December, 1880. He moved to the UK in 1901, and then, in 1923, he went to the USA to teach at the University of Pennsylvania. Later, he became a professor at Harvard Business School. He became interested in the effect of working conditions on productivity. He decided to conduct some experiments. There was nothing very original about the experiments themselves but the results form the basis of Industrial Psychology to this day. Between 1924 and 1927, Mayo conducted experiments at the Hawthorne Works. He wondered if the level of light in the factory affected the productivity of the workers. He experimented with the lighting levels for three years, but he found no change in productivity. Mayo then decided to look at the effect of tiredness on productivity. He wondered if productivity increased if you gave workers regular rest breaks or if you reduced the length of the working day. I don't know if you have ever been into a factory. I remember once I had to visit a factory. It was incredibly noisy and, of course, noise all day makes you tired. So it was a reasonable assumption that factory workers would be tired.
So, anyway, getting back to the point ... between 1927 and 1932, Mayo conducted another experiment with a group of six girls in the Hawthorne Works. During those five years, Mayo and his researchers observed the girls at work and made changes to their rest breaks and their working hours. After each change, a researcher talked to the girls about the changes and listened to any complaints they had.

Presenter: **E Listen to the second part of the lecture, which gives details of the experiment.**
Female lecturer: Before the experiment started, the girls worked a 48 hour week. They had no rest periods during the day. They did not have a specific target for productivity, but on average, each girl produced 2,400 items a week. Mayo introduced five-minute rest breaks, one in the morning and one in the afternoon. Productivity went up. Mayo lengthened the rest breaks to ten minutes each. Productivity went up sharply.
Mayo introduced another four rest breaks, but the girls complained that their work rhythm was broken, and productivity went down slightly. These extra rest breaks were removed and productivity went up again. The girls were allowed to leave at 4.30 p.m. instead of 5.00 p.m. Productivity went up.
Then they were allowed to leave at 4.00 p.m. They were now working one hour a day less in total, but productivity did not go down.
Mayo concluded that tiredness did have an effect on productivity. He believed, at this point, that a shorter working day and regular rest breaks were the key to increasing productivity.

Presenter: **F Listen to the third part. Each time the lecturer stops, answer her question.**
Female lecturer: Before he closed the experiment, however, he decided to do one final thing. It is the thing that any good researcher would do in the circumstances. What did he decide to do? [PAUSE] He took all the changes away, but continued to observe the girls and talk to them. The girls went back to the same conditions as before the experiment started – a 48-hour week, no rest breaks. What happened? [PAUSE] Productivity went up again. In fact, at this point, the girls reached an all-time record of over 3,000 items per week. How can the results be explained? [PAUSE]

Presenter: G Listen to the fourth part. What is the Hawthorne Effect?

Female lecturer: Mayo concluded that this is what happened: during the experiments, the six girls became a team. They realized that the management was interested in their work and listened to their complaints. They also realized that the amount of work they did – their productivity – was noticed. Mayo decided that productivity is affected by the amount that a worker is involved in the production process. Before the experiment started, nobody talked to the girls about their work. They felt they were just part of the factory machine. They did not feel valued. They did their work, but they did not do anything extra. When Mayo's researchers started to talk to them about their work, they felt that someone was noticing them as people. They felt valued. They did their work better because now they were putting extra effort into it. This discovery – that workers need to feel valued as people – is so important in the field of Industrial Psychology that it has a name, taken from the factory. When workers increase productivity because managers value their work, it is called the Hawthorne Effect. One other point came out of the experiment. Mayo noticed that, although all the girls were making the same item, they each had their own particular way of doing it. To put it another way, they each had a personal way to make a boring job a little bit more interesting. Mayo realised that people need to organise their own work in a way that will be interesting to them. There's a funny story about this. A man was visiting a factory where they make jam tarts. You know, they are little pieces of pastry with some jam on them. And he spoke to one of the girls who was operating a machine. He said, 'What do you do?' And she said, 'I push this button and the strawberry jam comes out of here.' And he said, 'But doesn't that get boring?' And she said, 'No. When I get bored, I push that button instead and make some tarts with raspberry jam.' Where was I? Oh, yes. Mayo wrote about the results of the Hawthorne experiments in a book published in 1933. It was called *The Human Problems of an Industrial Civilization*. He went on to write two other books, in 1939 and 1947. He died on 1st September, 1949.
So we have heard about Elton Mayo and the Hawthorne Effect, the discovery that really started the idea of Industrial Psychology – or the way that people think about work.
Next week, I'm going to talk about two people and their theories about Industrial Psychology.

Presenter: Lesson 3: Learning new listening skills
A 2 Listen and check your ideas.

Voice: it all started with
to this day
in fact
in the circumstances
in other words
getting back to the point
on average
in total
at work
for example
to put it another way

Presenter: D 4 Listen to this part of the lecture again.

Female lecturer: Mayo then decided to look at the effect of tiredness on productivity. He wondered if productivity increased if you gave workers regular rest breaks or if you reduced the length of the working day. I don't know if you have ever been into a factory. I remember once I had to visit a factory. It was incredibly noisy and, of course, noise all day makes you tired. So it was a reasonable assumption that factory workers would be tired.
So, anyway, getting back to the point …

Presenter: 6 Listen to this part of the lecture again.

Female lecturer: One other point came out of the experiment. Mayo noticed that, although all the girls were making the same item, they each had their own particular way of doing it. To put it another way, they each had a personal way to make a boring job a little bit more interesting. Mayo realized that people need to organize their own work in a way that will be interesting to them. There's a funny story about this. A man was visiting a factory where they make jam tarts. You know, they are little pieces of pastry with some jam on them. And he spoke to one of the girls who was operating a machine. He said, 'What do you do?' And she said, 'I push this button and the strawberry jam comes out of here.' And he said, 'But doesn't that get boring?' And she said, 'No. When I get bored, I push that button instead and make some tarts with raspberry jam.' Where was I? Oh, yes.

Presenter: Lesson 4: Applying new listening skills
B Listen to the introduction.

Female lecturer: Last week, I talked about the start of Industrial Psychology, which is the study of how people think about work. I described the experiments of Elton Mayo at the Hawthorne Works, and the Hawthorne Effect, which says that people work better when they feel valued.
This week, two more writers in the field of Industrial Psychology. But before that, I'm going to mention the thing they have in common: motivation. In the end, Industrial Psychology is all about motivation at work. What motivates people to work hard – or not to work hard?
OK, so first, motivation. What is it? One definition is: a way of satisfying needs through action and behaviour. In other words, we need something, like money or food, and we try to get it. We are motivated by our needs. Researchers have discovered that different things motivate different people. Some people are motivated by very strange things. I remember once I met a boy who collected train numbers. Yes, that's right. The numbers of trains. Trains all look the same in Britain, but each one has an identification number. This boy travelled to railway stations and stood for hours writing down the train numbers in a notebook. If I said to most boys, 'Go and write down train numbers,' they would be very bored. But this boy was motivated to do it for fun.
Sorry. Where was I? Oh yes. Motivation. Different things motivate different people, so managers must understand the theories of motivation to get the best out of their employees.

Presenter: D Listen to the first part of the lecture. Make notes on the life of Maslow.

Female lecturer:	Right. So, let's look at some of the theories. Firstly, we have Abraham Maslow, spelt M-A-S-L-O-W. Maslow was born on April 1, 1908, in New York. He was one of seven children born to uneducated Russian parents. His mother and father pushed him very hard to succeed. He went to university in New York for some time and studied law. While he was still a student, he got married and moved to Wisconsin to continue his studies at the university there. He switched from law to psychology and got his BA in 1930, his MA in 1931 and his PhD three years later. He went back to New York to work as a teacher at a college. He wrote several books, including *Motivation and Personality* in 1943. In this book, he described his most famous theory – the hierarchy of needs. Maslow retired to California in his early 60s, and died there on June 8th, 1970.	Presenter: Female lecturer:	H 1 Look at Figure 1 again. Listen to the fourth part. Label each item in the figure either Hygiene factor (H) or Motivator (M). Herzberg knew about the work of Maslow, of course, but he developed a theory with a very important difference. Let's compare Herzberg's ideas with Maslow's. Look at Figure 1 again. Herzberg said Maslow's lower-level needs – physiological and safety – are not motivators. He called them 'hygiene' factors. Hygiene means keeping things clean. We teach children hygiene when we say, 'Wash your hands before you eat a meal. Clean your teeth after your meal.' Hygiene helps to prevent disease. In the same way, Herzberg said, a good salary and a safe place to work are just hygiene factors. They prevent workers being dissatisfied, but they don't motivate them. According to Herzberg, the motivators are the higher-level needs of Maslow's hierarchy – esteem and self-actualization. These are the things that make people work harder.
Presenter: Female lecturer:	F Listen to the second part of the lecture. Check your answers to Exercise E. As I just said, Maslow is best known for his Hierarchy of Needs. A hierarchy is a list of things in some sort of order – for example, important things at the top and less important things at the bottom. Maslow believed that inside every human being there are five needs. We can put them into a pyramid. Look at Figure 1 on your handout. At the base of the pyramid are the physiological needs – the needs for food, drink and a place to sleep. At the next level there are the safety needs. Above safety needs are social needs. These include the need for love and friendship. Next there is the need for esteem. People need to develop self-respect and to feel that other people respect them, too. At the top of the pyramid is an even more complicated idea. Maslow called it Self-Actualization. Put simply, this means achieving everything that you are capable of achieving. Not many people reach that level. This is why he has drawn the hierarchy as a pyramid. Maslow's key point about the hierarchy is this: a person is not motivated by higher level needs until the lower level needs have been satisfied. In other words, a person is not motivated by concerns for safety if he is hungry or thirsty. But once that need for food and drink is satisfied, it no longer motivates. Now, a person can only be motivated by greater safety in his life. And so on.	Presenter: Female lecturer:	I Listen to the fifth part. What does Herzberg's theory mean for managers? It means they must make sure all the hygiene factors are in place, but they must also make sure that employees are valued as people. There's quite a good story about this. A man sees three people working on a building site. He says to the first man, 'What are you doing?' The man says, 'I don't know. I just work here.' He asks the second man. He says, 'I'm cutting these stones so they are perfectly straight, and then I'm putting them on top of each other to make a perfect wall.' And he says to the third man, 'What are you doing?' And the third man says, 'I'm helping to build this mosque.' What does that story tell us? The first man is not motivated to work hard. The second man is working hard, perhaps, but for his own satisfaction. He doesn't see how his work fits into the whole job. The third man knows how important his job is. He is motivated because he sees the value of his work. OK. We've run out of time. More next week …
Presenter: Female lecturer:	G Listen to the third part of the lecture. Make notes on the life of Herzberg. OK. So that's Abraham Maslow. The second writer I want to talk about today is Frederick Herzberg, that's H-E-R-Z-B-E-R-G. Herzberg was a psychologist. He was born on April 18th, 1923, in the United States. His parents were poor, like Maslow's, and, like Maslow's, they were immigrants, from Lithuania, which in the 1920s was part of Russia. Herzberg did very well at school and, when he was 16, he won a place at college. While he was there, he got married, in 1944. He got his BS in 1946, his MS in Industrial Psychology in 1949 and his PhD the following year. He worked as a manager of a research laboratory from 1951 to 1957, and then became a professor of psychology at a university in Ohio. Herzberg wrote several books, including *Motivation to Work* in 1959. In this book, he described his famous theory of satisfiers and dissatisfiers. He died on January 19th, 2000.	Presenter: Voice:	Section 2: Speaking Lesson 1: Vocabulary for speaking C Read and listen to the article. Complete it with a green word in each space. Make any necessary changes. The dictionary defines conflict as 'a fight or struggle between two people or two groups of people'. There are conflict situations at home between husbands and wives and parents and children. There are conflict situations at school among students or between students and teachers. There are conflict situations at work, among workers or between workers and managers. Charles Handy, the British writer on management, believes we all need to know how to handle conflict, not just in business but in our own social lives, too. In his book *Understanding Organizations* (1985), he writes: 'An understanding of the possible sources of conflict and the strategies for handling conflict are essential to effective management in organizations and even to individual survival.' In other words, Handy believes we need to understand the possible causes of conflict and how to deal with it, as a manager in an organization and as a person in daily life. If we are slow at dealing with conflict, the

	results can be very bad. A manager may dismiss a worker, a child may leave home, husbands and wives may separate. How do you handle conflict? Do you get angry and start an argument? Do you get upset? Or do you try to ignore the problem and hope that it will go away? What is the best way to behave?
Presenter:	**Lesson 2: Practising speaking** **A Read and listen to the case study on the right. What problem must you deal with in this case?**
Voice:	You are the manager of a small company called Allen's Construction. For years you worked with a small group of colleagues, but last month the previous manager left and you were offered the job. You accepted and the other workers were happy. At least, all of them were except Andreas. At first, when you asked him to do something, he often ignored your instructions. Then he started to argue every time. Just after lunch yesterday, you gave him a job to do and he shouted, 'Do it yourself. You shouldn't be the manager anyway. You only got the job because you are Mr. Allen's cousin.' Then he stormed out and went home. He has just arrived at work this morning. It seems that he has forgotten the argument. What should you do?
Presenter:	**F Read and listen to the article from Management Today.**
Voice:	In their book, *Developing Management Skills*, David Whetten and Kim Cameron talk about separating the person and the problem. They point out that people are not problems. People have problems. When there is conflict, it is easy to attack the person, not the problem. You say things like: You are stupid. You are always late. You are lazy. This is a mistake. Try not to use the verb be in an argument. We use be in statements of fact, to describe fixed or long-term situations, like You are French or You are eighteen. If you use You are … about a person's behaviour, it sounds like the person can never change. Concentrate instead on what happened: You forgot to give me the message. You arrived late three times last week. You didn't finish the work that I gave you. Talk only about actions. Don't mention facts or ideas that are not relevant. Then try to find out why the action happened and how to stop it happening again.
Presenter:	**Lesson 3: Learning new speaking skills** **B 2 Listen and check your ideas.**
Voice:	Are you for or against? Do it yourself. I always work hard. I saw a man. I'd like more of those. They all accepted. We often go there. Who opened the door? You asked me.
Presenter:	**Theme 4: Science and Nature, Dealing with the Weather** **Section 1: Listening** **Lesson 1: Vocabulary for listening** **A 2 Listen and check your answers.**
Voice:	The Sahara Desert occupies a third of the African continent. In fact, it occupies around eight per cent of the land area of the Earth. In total, it is about eight million square kilometres. It is expanding at the rate of about one kilometre a month. But the Sahara is not just sand. In fact, there are about 1,000 different types of plant.
Presenter:	**B 2 Listen and check your ideas.**
Voice:	The haboob is a turning sandstorm or duststorm. Its name comes from the Arabic word for strong wind. It can reach up to two kilometres wide and one kilometre high. It travels across the land at speeds of between 50 and 80 kilometres per hour. A haboob can last from one hour up to three hours. The haboob occurs mainly in the Sahara, but can also appear in the southwestern states of the United States. How does a haboob form? Air falls from thunderclouds in their final stage. When the falling air hits the ground, it picks up huge amounts of sand or dust. The wall of sand moves forward with the thunderclouds.
Presenter:	**Lesson 2: Practising listening** **D Listen to the first part of the talk.**
Roger Dawkins:	Today I'm going to talk about tornadoes. Firstly, I'm going to define a tornado. Secondly, I'm going to talk about the origins of the word. Then I'll tell you about the size, speed and duration of tornadoes. Next, I'll explain where they occur and when. After that, I'll describe two scales for measuring tornadoes. Finally, I'm going to talk about three theories that try to explain why tornadoes form.
Presenter:	**E Listen to the second part of the talk.**
Roger Dawkins:	So, first, what is a tornado? A tornado is a column of wind which is turning violently. The name comes from a Spanish word meaning 'thunderstorm'. The average tornado is 100 metres across – that's about the length of a football field – and it turns at 500 kilometres per hour – that's about four times as fast as the speed limit on a motorway. However, the magnitude and turning speed can vary enormously. Tornadoes can reach one kilometre across – that's 10 football pitches – and can turn at 800 kilometres per hour – that's the speed of a commercial aeroplane. By the way, don't confuse the turning speed with the travelling speed, that is the speed across the ground. Tornadoes travel quickly, but not at 500 kilometres an hour. They move across the land at about 50 kilometres an hour, although they can go two or three times that speed. I don't know if you saw that film of people trying to outrun a tornado in their car. They were filming a tornado in the distance when, suddenly, they realized that it was coming in their direction. It was very frightening, because the tornado caught up with them, even though they were driving very fast, but they kept filming out of the back of the vehicle, right up to the moment when they crashed the car. Nobody was hurt, thankfully.

Anyway, where was I? Oh, yes, size and speed can vary enormously. Similarly, the duration of tornadoes covers a wide range. Most only last a few minutes, but some go on for up to two hours.

Lastly, the distance they travel. Again, there's a big range – from about seven kilometres to over 200. Incidentally, some tornadoes can cause some very strange effects. Tornadoes do not contain rain, but things can fall out of the sky after a tornado. For example, a recent story comes from the town of Villa Angel Flores in Mexico. At 11 p.m. on June 2nd, 1997, small creatures began to fall on the town. They were toads – a kind of frog. The explanation came eventually. A tornado picked up the toads from a lake and dropped them several kilometres away on the town. So, if you hear an English person say, 'It's raining cats and dogs', he or she might be telling the truth! Actually, that's got nothing to do with tornadoes. Cats and dogs used to sleep on the roofs of houses, and when the roofs got very wet from heavy rain, they fell off … so people said, 'It's raining cats and dogs.'

OK, so tornadoes are columns of turning wind. Now let's see where they happen. Well, turning winds occur all over the world, but tornadoes are the most violent kind, and the destructive ones occur mostly in the United States. In fact, most of them happen in just one part of the United States, in an area of the central plains called Tornado Alley. The US experiences more than 500 tornadoes every year. There are also tornadoes in Western Europe, India, China, Japan and Australia. OK. We've heard that tornadoes occur in many parts of the world. But when do they occur? Summer or winter? Daytime or night-time? Morning or evening? Tornadoes can occur at any time of the day, in any month of the year. In the United States, however, three-quarters of tornadoes arise from March to July, with the majority in May.

Now let's consider how we can measure tornadoes. We can measure tornadoes on two main scales, the Fujita scale – that's F-U-J-I-T-A – and the Torro scale – T-O-R-R-O. Both scales classify the speed and destructive power of the tornado. The Fujita scale goes from 0 to 5, whereas the Torro scale runs from 0 to 12. On the Torro scale, one is mild; the wind will blow down small trees and blow off the tops of chimneys. Twelve is a super-tornado; the wind will move cars over 100 metres and even steel-reinforced buildings will be seriously damaged.

Presenter: **G 2 Listen to the third part of the talk.**

Roger Dawkins: So now we know what tornadoes are and where they occur. We also know how to measure them. But how do tornadoes form? There are three theories about this.

The first theory is the main one. It's called the Rising Air Theory. This theory says that tornadoes happen when a long column of quickly rising air stretches up from the ground. It often goes to a thundercloud. This can happen when the ground gets very hot and a bubble of air starts rising.

Now let's consider the second theory. The second theory is called the Downward Spiral Theory. This suggests that the tornado develops in a downward direction from a thunderstorm cloud to the ground. Finally, the third theory. This is the Electrical Storm Theory. I'm going to tell you a story to explain this theory. One day, in the middle of a storm, a farmer looked up into the heart of a tornado. What could he see? The farmer said the middle of the tornado was constantly lit by lightning flashes. So the Electrical Storm Theory says that lightning is the cause of tornadoes.

So, to sum up, we don't really know the exact cause of tornadoes. It could be rising air, a downward spiral or lightning.

That's all for this week. In next week's programme, we'll look at another violent turning wind – the hurricane.

Presenter **Lesson 4: Applying new listening skills**
Voice: **A 3 Listen and check your ideas.**
tornado
kilometres
violent
incidentally
electrical
develop
classify
damaged
seriously
destructive
vary
effects

Presenter: **C Listen to the first part of the talk.**
Roger Dawkins: Welcome to Violent Nature. Last week, I talked about tornadoes. This week, I'm going to talk about another powerful turning wind – the hurricane. Firstly, I'm going to explain what a hurricane is and tell you the origins of the name. Secondly, I'm going to tell you where and when they occur. Next, I'll describe some ways of measuring hurricanes. Finally, I'm going to talk about two theories that try to explain how hurricanes form.

Presenter: **D Listen to the second part of the talk.**
Roger Dawkins: So, first, what is a hurricane? Well, it's a turning wind, like a tornado, but there are two main differences between hurricanes and tornadoes. Firstly, hurricanes only start over water, whereas tornadoes only start over land. Secondly, hurricanes are huge rainstorms, whereas tornadoes don't have any rain in them. I suppose you could add a third difference. Hurricanes are much more destructive than tornadoes. In fact, hurricanes are the most destructive form of weather in the world. A hurricane that hit the American city of Galveston in 1900 is still considered to be the worst natural disaster in US history. More than 37,000 people died and 3,600 buildings were completely destroyed. Now there is more protection for people and buildings against hurricanes, but Hurricane Andrew, which hit the US in 1993, still killed 26 people and caused over 25 billion dollars worth of damage.

By the way, perhaps you have noticed that hurricanes always have the names of people – like Andrew. This practice started in Australia in the early 1900s. An Australian called Clement Wragge introduced the idea. It is said that he gave each hurricane the name of a person that he didn't like. Nowadays, a committee decides on the list of names for hurricanes. You can find the list of names for the next few years on www.fema.gov/kids/hunames.htm.

That's www dot f-e-m-a dot g-o-v forward slash kids forward slash h-u-n-a-m-e-s dot h-t-m.

Anyway, the name hurricane itself comes from Mayan – M-A-Y-A-N – the language of the tribes who lived in Mexico hundreds of years ago. Hurakan, spelt H-U-R-A-K-A-N was a god who breathed on the oceans and made dry land. Later, Indians who lived in the Caribbean used the name Hurican – H-U-R-I-C-A-N – as the name of an evil god, and many years later the University of Miami adopted the name, with a change in spelling, for any strong turning storm, that forms over warm water with winds above 119 kilometres an hour. OK, so hurricanes, like tornadoes, are turning storms. Now, let's see where they happen. Well, as I said just now, hurricanes form over warm water, so we don't get hurricanes in the Antarctic Ocean. In fact, the temperature of the air above the water must be more than 27 degrees centigrade, so the majority of hurricanes form in the tropics. In fact, there are six main areas, including the Western Atlantic, the Eastern Pacific and the South Indian oceans. Incidentally, you can see where the current hurricanes are all over the world if you go to www.solar.ifa.hawaii.edu. That's w-w-w dot s-o-l-a-r dot i-f-a dot hawaii dot e-d-u.

OK. So we've seen that hurricanes occur in many parts of the world. But when do they happen? Is there a hurricane season, in the same way as there is a tornado season? Well, the answer is 'yes and no'. Hurricanes generally happen in the summer, but the length of the hurricane season varies in each hurricane area. For example, the Atlantic hurricane season officially starts on June 1 and ends on November 30, but most tropical storms and hurricanes form between August 15 and October 15. By contrast, hurricanes occur year-round in the western North Pacific, while in the North Indian Ocean, there are two peaks of activity, in May and November.

Now let's consider how we can measure hurricanes. The most commonly used scale is the Saffir-Simpson scale. The scale runs from 1 to 5, with a Level 1 hurricane having winds of 119 to 153 kilometres per hour. This level causes minimal damage, mainly to trees and bushes. Level 5, on the other hand, has wind speeds of up to 270 kilometres an hour and causes catastrophic damage to buildings and great loss of life. By the way, don't be confused by the numbers on the Saffir-Simpson scale. A Level 5 hurricane is not five times as violent as a Level 1 hurricane. It's not even 50 times as violent. It is 500 times as violent.

Presenter: G **Listen to the talk again. Check your answers to the questions in Exercise F.**
[REPEAT OF LESSON 4, EXERCISE D]

Presenter: H **Listen to the final part of the talk. Draw a diagram showing the formation of hurricanes according to each theory.**

Roger Dawkins: So now we know what hurricanes are and where they occur. We also know how to measure them. But how do hurricanes form? There are two theories about this.

The first theory is the main one. It's called the Convection Theory. Convection, which is spelt C-O-N-V-E-C-T-I-O-N, means air moving upwards. Air starts to turn slowly over a tropical ocean. Hot air inside rises. More air is sucked in at the bottom and that air rises, too. The air on the outside starts to turn more quickly. This process continues and grows until a hurricane is formed. The hurricane continues to grow until it moves over land or over cooler water.

Now let's consider the second theory. It is called the Electromagnetic Theory. Some scientists believe that hurricanes occur when the Earth gets closer to the sun. This happens from June to November every year. According to this theory, the sun has an influence on part of the Earth's atmosphere, which causes areas of low pressure. These areas produce clouds and electrical storms. The electrical activity starts a turning wind and, eventually, a hurricane forms.

So, to sum up, most people believe that hurricanes form when more and more air is sucked up in organized convection, but some people believe electrical activity is the cause.

That's all for this week. Next week, we are going to look at some more forces of nature – not weather this time, but movements that start inside the Earth itself.

Presenter: **Section 2: Speaking**
Lesson 2: Practising speaking
B 1 **Read and listen to the text.**

Voice: How do animals survive in very cold or very hot climates? Over thousands of years, the animals we see today at the poles and in the desert have adapted to temperatures below -80°C and above 50°C. There are three main ways in which animals have adapted:
behaviour – they behave in a particular way
physical features – size or shape of body or parts of it
body functions – their organs work in a particular way

Presenter: **Lesson 3: Learning new speaking skills**
A 3 **Listen to the pairs of words.**
Voice:
a	hibernate	hibernation
b	adapt	adaptation
c	identify	identification
d	insulate	insulation
e	classify	classification
f	migrate	migration
g	condense	condensation
h	evaporate	evaporation

Presenter: C **Read and listen to the conversation.**
A: In winter, the wood frog goes into hibernation.
B: What does hibernation mean?
A: It means the animal stops breathing and the heart stops.
B: Why do animals … what's the verb?
A: Hibernate.
B: How do you pronounce it?
A: 'Hibernate. Stress the first syllable.
B: Why do animals hibernate?
A: Because there is not enough food.
B: I see. Carry on.
A: Well, the frog's blood falls below freezing point. But the blood doesn't actually freeze.
B: Why not?
A: Because the frog has a special chemical in its blood.
B: Sorry. I don't understand the part about the blood.
A: The frog produces a kind of antifreeze – like in a car engine.
B: Oh, right.

Presenter: Theme 5: The Physical World, Geology
Section 1: Listening
Lesson 1: **Vocabulary for listening**
B Listen and look at the pictures. Copy the green words and phrases into one or both columns.

Voice: There are many similarities between earthquakes and volcanoes. Both can cause natural disasters. When an earthquake occurs in a town or city, the earth shakes violently, and this can cause a lot of damage to buildings. This often leads to many deaths. In a similar way, when a volcano erupts near a town or city, the hot rocks and ash can damage buildings and kill people. Both kinds of event can also cause tidal waves. In fact, tidal waves after earthquakes or volcanic eruptions often cause more damage than the original event. There are also some differences between earthquakes and volcanoes. Earthquakes usually only last for a few seconds or minutes, whereas volcanoes can erupt for days or even months. With a volcano, fire often shoots high into the air, while earthquakes are not usually linked with fire from underground. Of course, damaged buildings often catch fire after an earthquake.

Presenter: Lesson 2: **Practising listening**
A Listen to the introduction. What exactly are you going to hear about in this lecture?

Female lecturer: There are two natural disasters that have killed millions of people in the history of the Earth. One shakes the ground, the other explodes and sends rocks and fire out of the ground. We call the first one an earthquake. We call the second one a volcano. For centuries, people believed there was a relationship between earthquakes and volcanoes. Do earthquakes cause volcanoes? Do volcanoes cause earthquakes? Or does something else cause both of them? This week, we are going to look at earthquakes, next week we will look at volcanoes, and by the end of the two lectures you should be able to answer the question: What is the relationship between these two terrible natural disasters?
So this week we are going to hear about early theories of the cause of earthquakes, and then we are going to hear about a famous earthquake that led to scientific research in Europe. We are then going to hear how the real cause of earthquakes was finally discovered.

Presenter: C Listen to the first part of the lecture.
Female lecturer: Thousands of years ago, people believed that there were huge animals that lived underground. Some people thought they were snakes, others believed they were turtles. Some even said they were giant spiders. According to these people, the animals sometimes got angry and when they did, the earth shook. Aristotle, the famous Greek philosopher of the 4th century BCE, did not believe in giant underground animals. His explanation was almost as strange, though. He thought there were huge winds under the earth that sometimes caused the ground to shake. In fact, the Greek word for 'shaking' is seismos – S-E-I-S-M-O-S. Eventually, therefore, the science of earthquakes became known as seismology.

Presenter: D Listen to the second part of the lecture.
Female lecturer: The earliest recorded earthquake was in 1177 BCE in China, but scientists in Europe were not interested in earthquakes until around 1750 CE. At that time, earthquakes started to shake England. This was very unusual, and the English scientists of the day became interested in them. These small earthquakes were warnings of a much bigger earthquake. On Sunday November 1st, 1755, a huge earthquake hit the city of Lisbon, in Portugal. The earthquake, and the tidal wave that followed it, flattened the city and killed around 70,000 people. There were eyewitness accounts of the terrible scenes. One wrote:
'We began to hear a rumbling noise, like that of carriages, which increased to such a degree as to equal the noise of the loudest cannon; and immediately we felt the first shock, which was succeeded by a second and a third; on which, as on the fourth, I saw several light flames of fire issuing from the sides of the mountains, resembling that which may be observed on the kindling of coal ... I observed from one of the hills called the Fojo that there issued a great quantity of smoke, very thick, but not very black which still increased with the fourth shock, and after continued to issue in a greater or less degree. Just as we heard the underground rumblings, we observed it would burst forth at the Fojo; for the quantity of smoke was always proportional to the underground noise.'
Anyway, after the Lisbon earthquake, scientists in Europe realized that earthquakes could be very dangerous, and they began to record the times and locations of earthquakes. They also began to work on ways of measuring earthquakes. As communications between countries got better, scientists in Europe began to collect observations from places as far away as South America and Japan. In the early 19th century, scientists suspected that there was something about the geology or type of rock in particular places that led to earthquakes.

Presenter: E 2 Listen to the third part and check your ideas.
Female lecturer: In the 1850s, the first true seismologist appeared, a man called Robert Mallet, and in 1880 the first instrument for measuring earthquakes was invented, by a man called John Milne, while he was working in Japan. He called it a seismograph.
In the United States, a man called Gilbert studied the rocks after an earthquake and decided that the lines he found in the rocks came before the earthquake, not after it. These lines were called faults. Similarly, a man called Reid studied fault lines in rocks after the 1906 San Francisco earthquake. He concluded that pressure builds up along a fault line and is eventually released as an earthquake.

Presenter: F 2 Listen to the fourth part and check your ideas.
Female lecturer: What is a fault line? How does it occur? If you look at a map showing the main earthquake areas, you can see immediately that earthquakes are more common in some places than others. Why is this? In the 1920s, a German meteorologist and astronomer named Alfred Wegener proposed a startling theory. He said the continents were not fixed in their position on the globe. Instead, they were moving around on huge plates. In some places, the plates come together. This is where earthquakes happen. At first, other scientists laughed at his ideas, but gradually, people found more and more evidence for his plate theory.

Presenter:	**G** Listen to the fifth part and draw a diagram from the information.
Female lecturer:	We now know that Reid's conclusion about earthquakes and fault lines is correct. The main cause of earthquakes is the movement of the rocks along fault lines where two continental plates meet. One plate is trying to move north, for example. The other plate is trying to move south. Friction between the rocks on each plate prevents this from happening. Pressure builds up, until finally, the rocks slide against each other. We call this an earthquake. There are more than 100 earthquakes a day. Incidentally, if you want to see the location of current earthquakes, go to www.gps.caltech.edu and follow the links to earthquakes and records of the day. How do the plates move? Actually, the solid rock that we see on the surface of the Earth is lying on a layer of very soft rock. The plates can slide on this soft rock. Very, very slowly, but they can slide. So, in a strange way, Aristotle was almost right about earthquakes. There are no winds under the ground to move the rocks around, but there is a kind of river that is moving all the time – a river of soft rock.

Presenter:	**Lesson 3:** Learning new listening skills **A 3** Listen and check your ideas.
Voice:	a Some people thought they were snakes, others believed they were turtles. Some even said they were giant spiders. b Aristotle thought there were huge winds under the earth that sometimes caused the ground to shake. c After the Lisbon earthquake, scientists in Europe realized that earthquakes could be very dangerous. d In the early 19th century, scientists suspected that there was something about the geology in particular places that led to earthquakes. e Gilbert decided that fault lines in rocks came before the earthquake, not after it. f Reid concluded that pressure builds up along a fault line and is eventually released as an earthquake. g Wegener proposed a startling theory.

Presenter:	**C 1** Listen to the first signposts from the lecture in Lesson 2. Can you remember how the lecturer continues in each case?
Female lecturer:	1 One plate is trying to move north, for example. 2 Some people thought there were snakes underground. 3 The continents were not fixed in their position on the globe. 4 At first, other scientists laughed at Wegener's ideas, …

Presenter:	**2** Listen and check your ideas.
Female lecturer:	1 One plate is trying to move north, for example. The other plate is trying to move south. 2 Some people thought there were snakes underground. Other people believed there were turtles. 3 The continents were not fixed in their position on the globe. Instead, they were moving around on huge plates. 4 At first, other scientists laughed at Wegener's ideas, but gradually people found more and more evidence for his plate theory.

Presenter:	**3** Listen to some more first signposts. What will come next?
Voice:	1 On the one hand, I want to go out this evening. 2 One parent wants his son to be a doctor. 3 Some people like meat. 4 I did not wait for the person to call me. 5 At first, nobody believed him, …

Presenter:	**Lesson 4:** Applying new listening skills **A 3** Listen and check your ideas.
Voice:	natural disaster explodes earthquake volcano observations communications geology eventually evidence concluded meteorologist

Presenter:	**C** Listen to the introduction.
Female lecturer:	Last week we looked at earthquakes and we saw that they are caused by the movement of the continental plates. This week, we are going to look at another natural disaster, volcanoes. We are going to consider a number of questions. What is the origin of the name? When and where was the most famous volcanic eruption? Why is it famous? How do volcanoes appear? How long do they take to form? And finally, what is the relationship between earthquakes and volcanoes?

Presenter:	**D** Listen to the first part of the lecture.
Female lecturer:	The word 'volcano' comes from the name of a small island in the Mediterranean Sea. Hundreds of years ago, people living in the area noticed fire coming out of the mountain on the island. They believed that the mountain was the chimney of a blacksmith's shop owned by a man called Vulcan. A blacksmith is a person who works with hot metal to make shoes for horses and metal objects like swords. According to legend, Vulcan the blacksmith made weapons for Mars, the Roman god of war. So, some people believed volcanoes were the flames from underground fires. Others thought there was fire under the whole of the Earth. Aristotle, as we have heard, said there were winds rushing around under the Earth. These winds caused earthquakes and, when they broke through the Earth, they caused volcanoes.

Presenter:	**E 3** Listen to the second part and check or complete the table.
Female lecturer:	What is the most famous volcanic eruption? Well, you have probably heard of it. It occurred in Italy in 79 CE. On that day, the volcano Vesuvius erupted. It destroyed several places, including the city of Pompeii. But why is the eruption so famous? Firstly, the event was described by Pliny the Younger in two letters. In his eyewitness account he wrote: The cloud was rising from Vesuvius. I can best describe its shape by likening it to a pine tree. It rose into the sky on a very long 'trunk' from which spread some 'branches.' Some parts of the cloud were white; other parts were dark with dirt and ash ….

Meanwhile, broad sheets of flame were lighting up many parts of Vesuvius; their light and brightness were the more vivid for the darkness of the night. The buildings were being rocked by a series of strong tremors, and appeared to have come loose from their foundations and to be sliding this way and that. Outside, however, there was danger from the rocks that were coming down …

As the column of ash rose over 30 kilometres, and over 3,000 people died, Pliny watched and wrote his account of the eruption.

However, Pliny's eyewitness account was not enough to ensure that Pompeii went down in history. In fact, the story of the eruption was completely forgotten over the years, and Pompeii lay buried under metres of ash. Then, the city was rediscovered. A small amount of excavation happened in the early 1800s, then, in 1860, an archaeologist called Giuseppe Fiorelli – that's F-I-O-R-E-L-L-I, became director of the excavations. Fiorelli realized that the bodies under the ash had completely disappeared but had left empty spaces. He poured plaster into the empty spaces, then dug away the ash. We can still see the result of his work today. One is a dog trying to get free from its chain at the moment of death. Another is a young man trying to protect an old woman from the falling ash. Incidentally, the eruption of Vesuvius is certainly not the earliest recorded volcanic eruption. Before the time of written language, someone painted a picture on the wall of a house in Catal Hayuk in modern-day Turkey. It shows a volcano erupting. Archaeologists have dated the painting to about 6200 BCE.

Presenter: F Listen to the third part of the lecture. Draw a diagram to show the modern theory of volcano formation.

Female lecturer: Anyway, where was I? Oh, yes. How do volcanoes appear? As we heard last week, scientists believe that there is a layer of soft rock under the hard rock at the surface of the Earth. The hard rock is moving around on the soft rock on huge continental plates. When the pressure builds at the meeting point of two plates, earthquakes occur. However, sometimes, when two plates meet, one plate is forced under the other plate. The plates rub together and friction turns the rock to a liquid called magma, spelt M-A-G-M-A. The plates continue to move and the pressure increases. Finally, the magma is forced to the surface and erupts out of the ground as a volcano.

Presenter: G Listen to the fourth part of the lecture. Make notes of the important information.

Female lecturer: How long does it take volcanoes to form? Most volcanoes form over millions of years. Some, however, appear and grow very quickly. I don't know if you have heard about the volcano that appeared in Mexico in 1943. A farmer in a place called Paricutin looked out of his window one day and saw that his donkey was standing on a small hill. This was strange, because the night before he tied the donkey to a tree in a flat field. He went and untied the donkey before the rope strangled him. Then he watched in amazement as the hill grew and grew.

Another farmer, Domini Pulido explained how the eruptions started:

'In the afternoon I heard a noise, like thunder during a rainstorm. At 4 p.m., I noticed that a small hole had opened in the ground. Then the ground raised itself two metres high, and a kind of smoke or fine dust – grey, like ashes – began to rise up. Immediately more smoke began to rise, with a hiss or whistle, loud and continuous, and there was a smell of sulphur. I then became greatly frightened.'

Anyway, the volcano at Paricutin grew to a height of 336 metres in the next year and began erupting the day after it first appeared. Eruptions continued for eight years and lava spread over an area of 25 square kilometres. By the way, lava is the name we give to the magma or liquid rock when it flows out of the volcano. So, the volcano at Paricutin grew in just eight years. Similarly, a volcano grew in the sea near Iceland in just four years. In fact, the volcano grew 130 metres from the seabed to the surface in just six months, from May to November 1963. At first, there were no eruptions. Then the volcano appeared above the surface, and it began to erupt. The lava eventually created a new island of three square kilometres and 170 metres at its highest point. Local people called the volcanic island Surtsey, after a fire giant in Icelandic stories.

Presenter: H 2 Listen and check your ideas.

Female lecturer: OK. So to sum up. Do earthquakes cause volcanoes? Do volcanoes cause earthquakes? No. Earthquakes do not cause volcanoes and volcanoes do not cause earthquakes. Instead, both earthquakes and volcanoes are caused by the movement of the continental plates. Incidentally, there are more than 1,500 active volcanoes in the world at the moment. You can see the latest information about eruptions if you go to http://volcano.und.nodak.edu – that's h-t-t-p-://v-o-l-c-a-n-o dot u-n-d dot n-o-d-a-k dot e-d-u – and follow the links to current eruptions. OK. Next week, we are going to talk about other natural disasters, like tidal waves and floods, and find out the cause of each.

Presenter: Section 2: Speaking
Lesson 1: **Vocabulary for speaking**
B 2 Listen and check your answers.

Voice: Around the centre of the Earth there is an imaginary line. We call it the Equator because there is equal area to the north and to the south of the line. The area on either side of the Equator is called the Tropics. The weather here is tropical, which means it is very hot and often very wet. At the very north of the Earth, we find the North Pole. The area around the North Pole is called the Arctic. At the very south of the Earth, we find the South Pole. The area around the South Pole is called the Antarctic.

Presenter: C 2 Listen and check your answers.
Voice 1: a The largest continent in the world is Asia, with an area of 44 million km^2.
Voice 2: b The largest country in the world is Russia, with an area of 17 million km^2.
Voice 3: c The wettest place in the world is Cherranpunji, India, with average rainfall of 1,270 cm p.a.
Voice 1: d The driest place in the world is the Atacama Desert in Chile in South America, with less than 0.01 cm p.a.
Voice 2: e The hottest place in the world is El Azizia, Libya, with a highest ever temperature of 57.8°C.
Voice 3: f The coldest place in the world is the South Pole, with a lowest ever temperature of –89.4°C.

Voice 1:	g	The largest desert in the world is the Sahara, with an area of 8.5 million km².
Voice 2:	h	The largest ocean in the world is the Pacific, with an area of 166 million km².
Voice 3:	i	The largest island in the world is Australia, with an area of 7.6 million km².
Voice 1:	j	The largest lake in the world is the Caspian Sea, Iran, with an area of 371,000 km².
Voice 2:	k	The longest mountain range is the Andes, South America, which is 7,200 km long.
Voice 3:	l	The highest mountain in the world is Mount Everest, which is 8,848 metres high.
Voice 1:	m	The longest river in the world is the Nile, which is 6,670 km long.
Voice 2:	n	The biggest river in the world is the Amazon, which has a delta with an area of 7 million km².
Voice 3:	o	The lowest point in the world is the Dead Sea, Jordan, which is 395 metres below sea level.

Presenter: **Lesson 2: Practising speaking**
A 2 Listen and check your answers.

Voice: lakes
seas
mountains
rivers
oceans
deserts
islands
countries

Presenter: B 2 Listen to the first part of the talk and check your answers.

Voice: I come from the continent of North America. [PAUSE]
The continent stretches from the Tropics in the south to the Arctic Ocean in the north. It is bordered by the North Atlantic Ocean in the east and the North Pacific Ocean in the west. [PAUSE]
People often think of North America as simply the United States, and perhaps Canada, but in fact there are 24 countries on the continent, including Mexico and Cuba, a large island off the southeast coast of the United States. [PAUSE]
The continent has two main mountain ranges. In the east are the Appalachians and in the west the Rockies. However, the highest point on the continent is not in the Appalachians or the Rockies. Instead, it is Mount McKinley, in the northwest of the continent. The mountain rises over 6,000 metres. [PAUSE]
There are many large rivers, including the St Lawrence and the Colorado, but the longest is the Mississippi-Missouri, which rises in the north of the United States and flows out of the Mississippi Delta into the Gulf of Mexico. The river is over 4,000 kilometres long. [PAUSE]
There are also many large lakes, including the series called the Great Lakes, on the border between the United States and Canada. [PAUSE]
There are several deserts in the southwest of the United States, including the Mojave. This desert contains the famous Death Valley, which is the hottest and driest location on the continent. [PAUSE]
There are many islands on the continent, including the West Indies, which is a large group of islands off the southwest coast of the United States. The West Indies are surrounded by the Caribbean Sea. [PAUSE]
The largest island on the continent is Greenland, in the extreme northeast. In fact, some people call this the world's largest island, because they say that Australia is a country, not an island. [PAUSE]

Presenter: D 2 Listen to the first part of the talk again and check or correct your labels.
[REPEAT OF LESSON 3 EXERCISE B2]

Presenter: E 2 Listen to the last part of the talk about North America. Write the colour of each climate region in the space provided.

Voice: North America is the only continent with all the climate types in the world.
As you can see from the map, in the far north we have the Arctic type, then the subarctic. Most of Canada has a tundra climate – that's the dark blue part – with low temperatures and no rainfall all year round. There are no trees. The eastern side of the United States – here – has a humid climate in the north, which means hot wet summers, and a humid subtropical climate in the south, which means very hot, wet summers. That's the orange part here. Most of the western side of the United States has a subtropical climate, dry and hot, with a large area of desert climate (the red part here), which is of course dry and very hot. Central America, in the Tropics here, has a wet tropical climate.

Presenter: **Lesson 4: Applying new speaking skills**
C Listen to a more detailed version of the talk from Lesson 2. Check your notes. Make more notes for other headings.

Voice: I come from the continent of North America. [PAUSE]
The continent stretches from the Tropics in the south to the Arctic Ocean in the north. It is bordered by the North Atlantic Ocean in the east and the North Pacific Ocean in the west. [PAUSE]
People often think of North America as simply the United States, and perhaps Canada, but in fact there are 24 countries on the continent, including Mexico and Cuba, a large island off the southeast coast of the United States. [PAUSE]
The largest country in the continent by area is Canada. It is nearly 10 million square kilometres. The United States is a little smaller, at just over nine million square kilometres. [PAUSE]
However, the United States is much bigger than Canada in terms of population. The country has more than 250 million people, compared with Canada's 27 million. [PAUSE]
The smallest country on the continent is called St Kitts and Nevis. That's S-T K-I-double T-S and N-E-V-I-S. It comprises two islands, with a total area of just 269 square kilometres. [PAUSE]
St Kitts and Nevis is also the smallest country in terms of population, with only 38,000 inhabitants. [PAUSE]
The continent has two main mountain ranges. In the east are the Appalachians and in the west the Rockies. However, the highest point on the continent is not in the Appalachians or the Rockies. Instead, it is Mount McKinley, in the northwest of the continent. The mountain rises over 6,000 metres. [PAUSE]
There are many large rivers, including the St Lawrence – that's S-T L-A-W-R-E-N-C-E and the Colorado – C-O-L-O-R-A-D-O, but the longest is the Mississippi-Missouri, which rises in the north of the United States and flows out of the Mississippi Delta into the Gulf of Mexico. The river is over 4,000 kilometres long. [PAUSE]

There are also many large lakes, including the series called the Great Lakes, on the border between the United States and Canada. The largest lake is called Lake Superior. It is over 80,000 square kilometres. [PAUSE]

There are several deserts in the southwest of the United States, including the Mojave. This desert contains the famous Death Valley, which is the hottest and driest location on the continent. Temperatures in Death Valley have reached 50 degrees centigrade. There is sometimes less than four centimetres of rain in one year. Death Valley is also the lowest point on the continent, at minus 86 metres, that is 86 metres below sea level. [PAUSE]

The wettest parts of the continent are in the northwest of the United States, near the border with Canada. This area has average rainfall of nearly 400 centimetres per year. [PAUSE]

There are many islands on the continent, including the West Indies, which is a large group of islands off the southwest coast of the United States. The West Indies are surrounded by the Caribbean Sea. [PAUSE]

The largest island on the continent is Greenland, in the extreme northeast. In fact, some people call this the world's largest island, because they say that Australia is a country, not an island. Greenland belongs to the European country Denmark. It has an area of more than 2 million square kilometres. The coldest place on the continent is in Greenland at North Ice, in the north of the island. [PAUSE]

WORD LISTS | Thematic

THEME 1
Education, Teaching and Learning

aural (adj)
brain (n)
doubled (adj)
forget (v)
kinaesthetic (adj)
learner (n)
link (v)
memorable (adj)
memory (n)
mode (n)
multiple (adj)
open (adj)
organize (v)
practice (n)
relevant (adj)
remember (v)
revise (v)
silent (adj)
visual (adj)
achieve (v)
assess (v)
behave (v)
behaviour (n)
discussion (n)
experience (n)
function (n)
grammar (n)
involve (v)
knowledge (n)
language (n)
learning (n)
listening (n)
observation (n)
observe (v)
point (n)
project (n)
pronunciation (n)
reading (n)
research (n)
role play (n)
skill (n)
speaking (n)
suppose (v)
theory/theories (n)
training (n)
vocabulary (n)
writing (n)

Words of your own:

_____
_____
_____
_____
_____
_____
_____
_____
_____
_____
_____
_____
_____
_____
_____
_____
_____
_____
_____
_____
_____
_____
_____
_____
_____
_____
_____
_____
_____
_____

THEME 2
Daily Life, Types of People

accept (v)
adult (n)
angry (adj)
apologize (v)
argue (v)
argument (n)
attitude (n)
behaviour (n)
calm (adj)
child/children (n)
colleague (n)
criticize (v)
deal with (v)
decision (n)
husband (n)
matter (n and v)
neighbourhood (n)
occasion (n)
optimistic (adj)
parent (n)
relationship (n)
response (n)
sorry (adj)
teenager (n)
trust (v)
upset (adj)
wife (n)
wrong (adj)
adolescence (n)
adolescent (n)
adulthood (n)
affect (v)
alternative (n)
appearance (n)
baby (n)
behave (v)
bring up (v)
change (mind) (v)
choose (v)
conflict (n)
decide (v)
decision (n)
develop (v)
effect (n)
environment (n)
factor (n)
genes (n)
genetics (n)
grow up (v)
heredity (n)
identity (n)
infancy (n)
infant (n)
inherit (v)
make up (mind) (v)
middle-aged (adj)
personality (n)
regret (n and v)
theory (n)

Words of your own:

_____
_____
_____
_____
_____
_____
_____
_____
_____
_____
_____
_____
_____
_____
_____
_____
_____
_____
_____
_____
_____
_____

THEME 3
Work and Business, Managing People

acronym (n)
administrator (n)
applicant (n)
balance (v)
colleague (n)
concentrate (v)
concentration (n)
conclude (v)
current (adj)
decide (v)
distract (v)
equal (v)
equation (n)
equipment (n)
evaluate (v)
furniture (n)
generate (v)
imagine (v)
increase (v)
organize (v)
previous (adj)
process (n)
purchase (v)
recommendation (n)
report (n)
resource (n)
select (v)
side (n)
solution (n)
TO DO list (n)
urgent (adj)
action (n)
advertise (v)
appoint (v)
cause (n)
colleague (n)
conflict (n)
decision (n)
dismiss (v)
employee (n)
experience (n)
flexible (adj)
handle (v)

ignore (v)
industrial (adj)
management (n)
manager (n)
need (n)
organization (n)
overtime (n)
process (n)
produce (v)
production (n)
promotion (n)
qualification (n)
recruitment (n)
reference (n)
reject (v)
rest break (n)
salary (n)
secure (adj)
security (n)
team (n)
worker (n)
working hours (n)

Words of your own:

_____
_____
_____
_____
_____
_____
_____
_____
_____
_____
_____
_____
_____
_____
_____
_____

THEME 4
Science and Nature, Dealing With the Weather

achieve (v)
aim (n)
animal (n)
around/about (= approx) (prep)
carbon (n)
climate (n)
construct (v)
convert (v)
cycle (n)
desert (n)
expand (n)
facts and figures (n)
fresh (water) (adj)
gas (n)
hydrogen (n)
liquid (n)
living thing (n)
nitrogen (n)
occupy (v)
oxygen (n)
plant (n)
polar (adj)
process (n)
project (n)
solid (n)
structure (n)
surface (n)
the Earth (n)
tropical (adj)
adapt (v)
amphibian (n)
backbone (n)
calculate (v)
cold-blooded (adj)
collect (v)
conclude (v)
cool (v)
duration (n)
energy (n)
feather (n)
formation (n)
fur (n)

gain (v)
heat (v)
insect (n)
insulate (v)
insulated (adj)
insulation (n)
lightning (n)
lose (v)
mammal (n)
measure (v)
observe (v)
occur (v)
origin (n)
predict (v)
reach (= max. amount) (v)
reptile (n)
sandstorm (n)
scale (n)
skin (n)
speed (n)
thunder (n)
timing (n)
warm-blooded (adj)
waste (v)

Words of your own:

_____
_____
_____
_____
_____
_____
_____
_____
_____
_____
_____
_____
_____
_____

WORD LISTS — Alphabetical

THEME 5
The Physical World, Geology

- agriculture (n)
- area (n)
- area (n)
- border (n and v)
- climate (n)
- continent (n)
- difference (n)
- different (adj)
- industry (n)
- location (n)
- main (adj)
- natural feature (n)
- neighbour (n)
- population (n)
- region (n)
- similarities (n)
- temperature (n)
- the economy (n)
- the same (adj)
- trading partner (n)
- damage (n and v)
- death (n)
- delta (n)
- desert (n)
- drill (v)
- energy (n)
- erupt (v)
- extraction (n)
- fire (n)
- form (v)
- fossil fuel (n)
- fuel (n)
- geologist (n)
- metal (n)
- mine (v)
- mining (n)
- natural disaster (n)
- ocean (n)
- petroleum (n)
- plastic (n)
- producer (n)
- product (n)
- range (n)
- rock (n)
- run out (v)
- shake (v)
- source (n)
- surface (n)
- the Antarctic (n)
- the Arctic (n)
- the North Pole (n)
- the South Pole (n)
- the Tropics (n)
- tidal wave (n)
- tropical (adj)
- underground (adj)
- well (n)

Words of your own:
_____
_____
_____
_____
_____
_____
_____
_____
_____
_____
_____
_____
_____
_____
_____
_____
_____
_____
_____
_____
_____
_____
_____

- accept (v)
- achieve (v)
- acronym (n)
- action (n)
- adapt (v)
- administrator (n)
- adolescence (n)
- adolescent (n)
- adult (n)
- adulthood (n)
- advertise (v)
- affect (v)
- agriculture (n)
- aim (n)
- alternative (n)
- amphibian (n)
- angry (adj)
- animal (n)
- apologize (v)
- appearance (n)
- applicant (n)
- appoint (v)
- area (n)
- argue (v)
- argument (n)
- around/about (= approx) (prep)
- assess (v)
- attitude (n)
- aural (adj)
- baby (n)
- backbone (n)
- balance (v)
- behave (v)
- behaviour (n)
- border (n and v)
- brain (n)
- bring up (v)
- calculate (v)
- calm (adj)
- carbon (n)
- cause (n)
- change (mind) (v)
- child/children (n)
- choose (v)
- climate (n)
- cold-blooded (adj)
- colleague (n)
- collect (v)
- concentrate (v)
- concentration (n)
- conclude (v)
- conflict (n)
- construct (v)
- continent (n)
- convert (v)
- cool (v)
- criticize (v)
- current (adj)
- cycle (n)
- damage (n and v)
- deal with (v)
- death (n)
- decide (v)
- decision (n)
- delta (n)
- desert (n)
- develop (v)
- difference (n)
- different (adj)
- discussion (n)
- dismiss (v)
- distract (v)
- doubled (adj)
- drill (v)
- duration (n)
- effect (n)
- employee (n)
- energy (n)
- environment (n)
- equal (v)
- equation (n)
- equipment (n)
- erupt (v)
- evaluate (v)
- expand (n)
- experience (n)
- extraction (n)
- factor (n)
- facts and figures (n)
- feather (n)
- fire (n)
- flexible (adj)
- forget (v)

58 RESOURCES BOOK LEVEL 3A – WORD LISTS

form (v)
formation (n)
fossil fuel (n)
fresh (water) (adj)
fuel (n)
function (n)
fur (n)
furniture (n)
gain (v)
gas (n)
generate (v)
genes (n)
genetics (n)
geologist (n)
grammar (n)
grow up (v)
handle (v)
heat (v)
heredity (n)
husband (n)
hydrogen (n)
identity (n)
ignore (v)
imagine (v)
increase (v)
industrial (adj)
industry (n)
infancy (n)
infant (n)
inherit (v)
insect (n)
insulate (v)
insulated (adj)
insulation (n)
involve (v)
kinaesthetic (adj)
knowledge (n)
language (n)
learner (n)
learning (n)
lightning (n)
link (v)
liquid (n)
listening (n)
living thing (n)
location (n)
lose (v)

main (adj)
make up (mind) (v)
mammal (n)
management (n)
manager (n)
matter (n and v)
measure (v)
memorable (adj)
memory (n)
metal (n)
middle-aged (adj)
mine (v)
mining (n)
mode (n)
multiple (adj)
natural disaster (n)
natural feature (n)
need (n)
neighbour (n)
neighbourhood (n)
nitrogen (n)
observation (n)
observe (v)
occasion (n)
occupy (v)
occur (v)
ocean (n)
open (adj)
optimistic (adj)
organization (n)
organize (v)
origin (n)
overtime (n)
oxygen (n)
parent (n)
personality (n)
petroleum (n)
plant (n)
plastic (n)
point (n)
polar (adj)
population (n)
practice (n)
predict (v)
previous (adj)
process (n)
produce (v)

producer (n)
product (n)
production (n)
project (n)
promotion (n)
pronunciation (n)
purchase (v)
qualification (n)
range (n)
reach (= max. amount) (v)
reading (n)
recommendation (n)
recruitment (n)
reference (n)
region (n)
regret (n and v)
reject (v)
relationship (n)
relevant (adj)
remember (v)
report (n)
reptile (n)
research (n)
resource (n)
response (n)
rest break (n)
revise (v)
rock (n)
role play (n)
run out (v)
salary (n)
sandstorm (n)
scale (n)
secure (adj)
security (n)
select (v)
shake (v)
side (n)
silent (adj)
similarities (n)
skill (n)
skin (n)
solid (n)
solution (n)
sorry (adj)
source (n)

speaking (n)
speed (n)
structure (n)
suppose (v)
surface (n)
team (n)
teenager (n)
temperature (n)
the Antarctic (n)
the Arctic (n)
the Earth (n)
the economy (n)
the North Pole (n)
the same (adj)
the South Pole (n)
the Tropics (n)
theory/theories (n)
thunder (n)
tidal wave (n)
timing (n)
TO DO list (n)
trading partner (n)
training (n)
tropical (adj)
trust (v)
underground (adj)
upset (adj)
urgent (adj)
visual (adj)
vocabulary (n)
warm-blooded (adj)
waste (v)
well (n)
wife (n)
worker (n)
working hours (n)
writing (n)
wrong (adj)